"Darren Main uses the simple tale of *The Wizard of Oz* to explain the simple truths of the perennial philosophy. This book is a clear and inspiring roadmap for the spiritual journey."

**Tom Moon, MFCC**
Psychotherapist, columnist, *San Francisco Frontiers*

"Delightfully written by Darren Main, *Spiritual Journeys Along the Yellow Brick Road* contains great pearls of spiritual wisdom as well as practical suggestions to speed us along our own yellow brick road. In this simple and insightful book, Main interprets the beloved classic, adding depth and meaning to its story as a metaphor for the spiritual journey."

**Christian de la Huerta,**
author of *Coming Out Spiritually*

"I loved the book on many levels. It deepened and enriched one of my favorite stories which has been an important legacy to our family for all of my life. As a student of Transpersonal Psychology, it appealed greatly to my passion for exploring many different spiritual truths. As a parent, I found this to be a great book for a generation of young people who have not been indoctrinated into a formal religion and who are looking for more meaning in their life...

Thank you, Darren, for your keen insights and personal examples, your ability to make meaningful connections between the story and universal archetypes and the freshness of your writing style. Your book will become a permanent part of my library."

**Janet Winters-Smith**
Grandaughter of Brenda and Harry Meal Baum
(son of *L. Frank Baum*)

"Darren John Main reveals a remarkable breadth of knowledge of many of the world's historic spiritual movements in his analysis of *The Wizard of Oz*. His analysis of the archetypal significance of the main characters as presented in the MGM classic movie—the version of L. Frank Baum's work most widely known throughout the world—will resonate for many readers."

**Peter E. Hanff**
President, *The International Wizard of Oz Club*

D0201543

# Spiritual Journeys along the Yellow Brick Road

Darren John Main

FINDHORN
Press

First published 2000

ISBN 1 899171 23 1

British Library Cataloguing-in-Publication Data.
A catalogue record for this book is available from the British Library.

Library of Congress Catalog Card Number: 99-67786

Cover design by Jasper Trout
Book layout by Thierry Bogliolo

Printed and bound in the USA

Published by

**Findhorn Press**

The Press Building, The Park
Findhorn, Forres IV36 3TY
Scotland, UK
tel 01309 690582
fax  01309 690036

P.O. Box 13939
Tallahassee
Florida 32317-3939, USA
tel 850 893 2920
fax 850 893 3442

info@findhornpress.com
**findhornpress.com**

# Contents

Dedicated to my beloved teacher, Jesus, whose life example and simple wisdom have shown me that the Peace of God is possible. Thank You so much for reminding me that Kansas is within.

## About L. Frank Baum

*by Eric Gjovaag*

Born in Chittenango in upstate New York on May 15, 1856, Lyman Frank Baum was the son of wealthy parents. He had a happy childhood, but Frank (he hated his first name, Lyman, and was known as Frank all his life) was a dreamer, and for a while was not much of a success at anything. He tried acting, selling machine oil and crockery, managing department stores, and newspaper editing and reporting, but nothing seemed to work very well for him, or hold his interest for long. He finally started writing when his mother-in-law encouraged him to write down the fanciful tales he'd been telling his four sons and their friends for years. Although he initially had trouble finding a publisher, his works eventually caught the fancy of the public, and he was able to finally make a decent living. Although he also dabbled in play production and the fledgling motion picture industry, he kept on writing until his death on May 6, 1919.

Photograph of L. Frank Baum by courtesy of The International Wizard of Oz Club. Originally published in *The Baum Bugle*. Photograph provided by William Stillman, Editor-in-Chief, *The Baum Bugle*, PO Box 266, Kalamazoo, MI 49004-0266.

# Acknowledgements

There are so many people who have influenced this book—from the homeless people on Castro Street to chance meetings on airplanes. There is no way I could remember them all, but you all have my deepest appreciation. There are a few people however, whose contributions I can place my finger on, and I would like to acknowledge them here.

L. Frank Baum—Thank you for giving us Oz and for planting the seeds of wisdom in the hearts and minds of children and adults alike. I pray that your soul is zipping around that cosmic Kansas in the sky and that your writing will continue to inspire us for generations to come.

Sue Louiseau— My San Francisco mom. Thank you so much for all your hard work, your great spelling, and your faith in me. I draw on your strength more than you will ever know. I am proud of all you have done with your life. I pray that you will never forget how beautiful you look in your ruby slippers!

Kathy Flynn-Ascare—My beautiful "Mumzy". You have walked through the thick and the thin with me. You have been a friend and a mother, and you have shown me that unconditional love is possible in this world. Your support in all of my crazy adventures, including the writing of this book, has helped me to unfold my wings and soar! There are just not enough wet hair hugs to thank you.

I would also like to acknowledge the following: Thierry and Karin Bogliolo at Findhorn Press, your faith in me will never be forgotten. Tony Mitton, for a great job editing with compassion and honesty. John Main, for the gift of integrity. Jason and Jennifer, for walking through childhood and beyond with me. Don and Adelina, for making my parents smile. Michael Lynch, for 50 Hillside Ave. Arthur Leiper, for reminding me that it goes against the grain. The Flynns and the Mains for bringing yin and yang to my life in such a balanced way. Jasper Trout, for opening my heart. Lance Johnson, for dancing with me on Baker Beach. Brian Lyttle, for sharing my sarong. Dan Tauntenhan, for dude. John Amodio, for being Mother Hartford. Schooner and Macy, for being more human than most people I know. Eve Nardone, for inspiring me to write and following me to meetings. Michael and Lizza for ACIM groups that rock. Lance King, for always questioning my statements and helping me to be grounded in my truth. Becky Holland

and Jen Dyer, for surviving SHS with me—I couldn't have done it alone. Charlie Schlegel, for helping me move mountains, not to mention furniture. Harry and Mary, Dorothy, Sheila, Megan and all the beautiful souls in Montana who welcomed me with open arms and continue to send me such love and support. Ed Gregory, for 24 Messer Street. Jackie Heart, for pickles & folk music. Sheri, for great pasta and truffles. Roy, for bagels, sunflowers and Drano. Christopher Love, for sharing our unique brand of humor. Marion Linsig, for Bish-Bash Falls. Kit Codik, for being my brother. Saint Brennan Claybaugh, for reminding me that we not only survive when we make difficult choices, we flourish. Bodhi Maisha, for helping me to see through a child's eyes—as you have grown up, so have I. David Nelson, for having vision and wisdom and trusting in our dream! The Castro Yoga staff, for helping to create an Emerald City in the heart of San Francisco. Bhakti Pratt, for reminding me to keep my buttocks firm. Megan Stohr, for traveling the landscape of this beautiful world with me. Craig Joiner, *Live long and prosper.* Apple Computer, for making this book possible, in the technical sense at least. The Sunday Night Meditation group in Providence—may we all find ourselves naked in a rain puddle sometime soon! And most importantly, my students, who are, in fact, not my students but my teachers. You have kept me in check, humbled me, and kept it all fresh and new. Without you I would hate to think where I would be today.

## Trademarks and Disclaimer

# Introduction

Have you ever been walking through the woods with a few friends and had everyone spontaneously break into the now famous "Lions and tigers and bears" chant? I think most of us have. *The Wizard of Oz* is a cultural phenomenon. It is as much a part of Western culture as stories about Santa Claus and the Easter Bunny.

In a sense, Oz is a true story. Of course it did not literally happen as a historical event any more than the Garden of Eden story did. But Oz is true. It conveys a universal spiritual message that is beyond time, beyond culture, and beyond belief and dogma.

Oz and all its colorful and animated characters are a system of archetypes that speak to a very deep part of our mind. This deep level of our psyche is uncharted territory for most of us, but one of the qualities of this level of consciousness is that it doesn't use words to express itself.

It uses symbols and images which represent patterns and beliefs that are fundamental to that which we are as human beings.

An archetype, therefore, is a symbol—in much the same way that the trash can icon is a symbol on the desktop of my Macintosh monitor. There is not literally a trashcan on my desktop. In fact there isn't even a desktop, but these symbols are things that everyone can identify with. Knowing almost nothing about a computer, it's easy to figure out that the things you drag into the trash are things you want to get rid of. No words are used, but a basic truth about computing has been conveyed.

The same is true for the Oz story. We can identify with Dorothy and her search for home because we are all trying to do the exact same thing. We may not be conscious of it, but we all have a deep longing to find "home". Likewise we feel at times as if we are not smart enough, like Scarecrow, or we experience fear paralyzing us in much the same way as the Lion.

By examining *The Wizard of Oz* from this perspective, I believe we can gain valuable insights into our own spiritual search for "Kansas". I believe we can learn from Dorothy's lessons and avert major roadblocks that would otherwise have kept us stuck. I also believe that by examining this epic story, we can learn our own lessons more easily, because the lesson plan is laid out before us. My friend Sheri always says, "God can teach us our lessons with a carrot or a stick." It is my hope that Oz will be one such carrot.

Before we can really explore the deeper meanings present in "Oz," I think it would be useful to talk about where this story came from. L. Frank Baum wrote the first "Oz" book in 1900, calling it *The Wonderful Wizard of Oz*. It met with a great deal of success and he further authored 13 more books and a number of short stories based on the

Land of Oz. Since his death various authors have published over 40 books on the subject.

In 1939 MGM studios released the now classic movie starring Judy Garland that was based on Baum's first book. Needless to say the movie was a great success and has become one of the most watched movies of all times.

In addition to the MGM classic, several movies have been made, including *The Wiz* and *A Return To Oz*, although none of them has risen to the level of the 1939 movie. Recently, rumors have surfaced on the Internet that Disney studios are talking about remaking the movie. If they do, it will be curious to see how it fares.

Baum is somewhat of a mystery man, as he seemed to have many different faces. It seems as though every text I read about the genius who created Oz is different. One thing is for certain though. Baum was not just trying to tell a story; he was trying to teach his children important lessons about life.

Many believed Baum to be a political man with each of the images contained in his Oz books representing various aspects of the political climate at the time the books were written. The most notable was a paper written by a teacher named Henry Littlefield, called *The Wizard of Oz: A Parable on Populism.*[1]

Others, myself included, believe Baum was a deeply spiritual man, and that his writing was inspired by his deeply held beliefs. According to a paper entitled *Oz, L. Frank Baum's Theosophical Utopia*[2], by David B. Parker, Baum was part of a spiritual renaissance, the wider implications of which we are starting to see today. According to Parker,

---

[1] American Quarterly magazine (1964).
[2] The article can be read in its entirety at the following web site: http://ksumail.kennesaw.edu/~dparker/oztheos.html

Baum was a Theosophist. And it was his Theosophical beliefs that were the seed for his writings.

To gain a deeper insight into Baum's spiritual beliefs and practices, I looked into Theosophy to learn more about what it espouses. One website[3] I found had this to say:

*The Secret Doctrine establishes three fundamental propositions. These basic ideas are few in number and on their clear apprehension depends the understanding of the philosophy of Theosophy.*

*FIRST,*

*There is One Infinite Principle which is the Cause of all that was or ever shall be. This causal Self is not absent from any point of space, and we are inseparable from it. We are, in essence, THAT which is unchangeable and unchanging. Behind all perceiving and knowing and experiencing is the One undivided Self. The power in us to perceive, to know, to experience—apart from anything that is seen, known or experienced—is the One Self, the one Consciousness, shared by all alike, the power of every being. Herein lies the true basis of Brotherhood—the unifying bond for all above man and for all below man.*

*SECOND,*

*The second idea—Law, is called Karma. It is the law of recurring cycles in Nature and the constant tendency to restore disturbed equilibrium. Karma applies to our moral*

---

[3] http://theosophycompany.org/

nature; it is the law of ethical causation, of justice, reward and punishment, the cause of birth and rebirth. Viewed from another standpoint, it is simply effect flowing from cause, action and reaction, the result of every thought and act. Karma means, literally, action. Theosophy views the universe as an intelligent whole, and every motion in the universe is an action leading to results, which themselves lead to further results. We always act in connection with others, affecting them for good or ill, and we get the necessary reaction from the causes set in motion by ourselves. This presents the idea of absolute justice and the essence of free-will.

Interwoven with Karma is another aspect of the law of cycles—Reincarnation. It means that men and women as thinkers, composed of soul, mind and spirit, occupy body after body in life on this earth which is the scene of our evolution, and where we must, under the laws of our being, complete that evolution. In any one life we are known as a personality, but in the whole stretch of eternity we are one individual, feeling in ourselves an identity not dependent on name, form or recollection.

THIRD,

The third fundamental principle points to the fact that all beings in the universe have evolved from lower points of perception into greater and greater individualization; that beings above man have gone through our stage; that there can never be a stoppage of evolution in an infinite universe of infinite possibilities; that whatever stage of perfection may be reached in any period there are always greater possibilities beyond.

Viewing life and its possible object, with all the varied experience possible for a human being, one realizes that a *single life is not enough for carrying out all that is intended by Nature, to say nothing of what we ourselves desire to do. The scale and variety in experience is enormous; every form of evolving intelligence in nature either was, is, or will be human.*

Interestingly enough, these were many of the principles I found as I began to contemplate the Oz story more deeply. Although I am not a Theosophist and know little of their beliefs, I can see where their teachings certainly influenced Baum's writing. And the universal nature of much of their beliefs is of great help in applying the imagery of Baum's work to our individual belief systems.

As far as this book is concerned, I had to make a somewhat difficult choice. Like most books that become films, there are many key areas where details get omitted or altered. The MGM movie is no exception. For example, in the book, Oz was a real place. It existed as much as China or India. It was very different than Kansas, but it was a place that anyone could travel to physically.

In the movie, Oz was a dream that Dorothy had. It was no more real than the dream I had last night about eating chocolate at the Joseph Schmidt Shop in San Francisco. In the movie, Dorothy woke up in the end, and like a regular dream, there was no real way to return. In the books that followed Baum's pilot, Dorothy did return and even took her family with her.

It is because of fundamental differences like this that I needed to make a choice. Which version of the story would I use as default—as the authority—when a discrepancy arose? Initially I chose the book because I felt (and still feel) that Frank Baum was an inspired writer. I believe that he was wise and that the book he offered the world was bigger than even he could have imagined.

But as I started to discuss my ideas with friends, they would say things like, "I thought her shoes were red"[4] or "I didn't know they had to wear glasses in the Emerald City." I realized that the archetypes that were set into our collective unconscious were set there largely by the MGM movie.

It is for this reason that I have chosen to write about the symbolism in the movie. This was a difficult decision for me because I really believe that Hollywood has butchered some of the greatest works ever put on paper. But after a great deal of reflection and meditation I settled into and became comfortable with my decision. In hindsight, I know I made the right choice.

To give proper credit in quotations, I will identify quotes that come from the movie with (MGM). When I use quotes from the book, I will follow the quote with (Baum).

One further note—this book is my interpretation of *The Wizard of Oz*. I bring to this book some life experiences and some study in Eastern and Western mysticism. This book is not the final word. My hope is that it will be a starting point and that each time you read or view *The Wizard of Oz* you will contemplate what it means for you.

I hope that this book will be for you a sign post as you travel along your yellow brick road.

— Darren

---

[4]In the book the shoes were silver. MGM is said to have changed the color to show off their color film.

# Chapter One

# The Yellow Brick Road

*"I'd give anything to get out of Oz altogether.*
*Which is the way back to Kansas? I can't go the way I came."*

—Dorothy Gale of Kansas (MGM)

*"It's always better to start at the beginning.*
*All you have to do is follow the yellow brick road."*

— Glinda, *Good Witch of the North* (MGM)

Just as a mother bird pushes her chicks out of the nest when they reach maturity, our Spirit gives us the gentle nudge to leave Munchkin Village and travel along our yellow brick road. For some a physical journey will be involved, while others will live near their childhood tribe for life. The journey along the yellow brick road is not to a destination, but rather a spiritual pilgrimage deep into the heart and psyche. When traveling along our yellow brick road, the journey is the destination.

The yellow brick road represents our path home. It is not so much a physical path as it is a center—a place to return to when we drift off course. The yellow brick road is not a dogma but neither is it a vast open plain filled with immorality and recklessness. It is the "middle path"[1]. And it provides structure and guidance as we try to find our heart's longing.

We begin our journey out of Munchkinland with our family, the Munchkins. Some souls will have the benefit of having their tribe escort them for part of the way, and others will not. But whether or not they back the soul on her quest, there will come a time when she needs to walk the path alone. It is at this point that a soul really begins to grow and develop. Dorothy begins to think for herself when she meets Scarecrow. She explores the vastness of her heart when she meets the Tin Woodsman, and she begins to develop faith and courage as she walks beside the Lion.

Like Dorothy, our path is sure to lead us through some interesting places—from the darkness of the Witch's castle to the radiance of the Emerald City. The yellow brick road takes us through all we need to see and introduces us to everyone we need to meet. It presents us with the lessons we need to learn and ultimately leads us back to Kansas.

Interestingly, it leads us to Kansas, not by showing us the way in any outward sense, but rather by teaching us that we do have power, that we can endure, and that all we ever needed already existed deep inside.

I am lucky. I work in a profession where I get to meet people on the "path" all day long. And what is most astounding is that every single person is walking a path as unique and unpredictable as the person walking it. Most

---

[1] The middle path is a Buddhist concept.

paths include some sort of prayer or meditation, a healthy and balanced moral code, and genuine respect for the body.

For many people, they start their journeys thinking that a spiritual journey will be a walk in the park, but walking the yellow brick road is often difficult because it means a commitment to truth. When we begin our journey, whether consciously or unconsciously, we ask our Spirit to show us all the areas that block our view of Kansas. We ask to be shown all the areas where we are judgmental. We request an honest appraisal of our life and we become willing to surrender to Spirit, knowing that we will be guided for our greater good.

Walking the yellow brick road means having the willingness to look at our values and beliefs and to let them go at a moment's notice. It means walking straight into the fire rather than dancing around the edges toasting little balls of fluff.

How else could it be? When you really think about it, we are unhappy and unfulfilled by the things in the world. We fill our time with activities that we think will bring us happiness or the wealth with which we can buy contentment, and it never works. We dream of the perfect mate or the perfect job or the great sex or the most satisfying food, but these things can never satisfy us—at least not in any lasting way.

The only way home is to walk swiftly "keeping tight inside our shoes."[2] There are no magic broomsticks to get us home quickly—only our deep commitment to trust in Spirit. As the Taoist saying goes, "The journey of a thousand miles begins with the first step," and this is exactly what we must do.

---

[2] MGM (see Chapter 4).

From time to time we may get distracted and wander from our path, but this is no cause for alarm. We will all wake up. We will all find our way. Like Dorothy, we are safe in Kansas. The dream will end; however, the quality and length of that dream will be largely up to us.

When a plane travels, it has a set flight plan. But quite often during the course of that flight, the plane drifts off course. In fact, if you looked at the flight records, you would find that the plane was almost never on course. The whole process of navigating the plane is one of drifting off course and then returning to center.

The soul is the pilot of your life, and the Spirit is its navigational system. Walking the yellow brick road is much like navigating a plane. When you find you have drifted off course, you simply allow your Spirit to guide you back.

And so we can choose to walk our paths consciously or unconsciously. We can choose to listen to the guidance of our Spirit, or we can ignore it. The yellow brick road is laid out before us to follow or stray from, to walk along or to sit at the curbside. As we make these choices, we evolve and grow, learning what works and doesn't work, and eventually we find our way home.

## Oz and Kansas

*"Oh, Toto, there's no place like home."*

—Dorothy (MGM)

For so much of my early life, I never seemed to fit in. In some social circles, I felt connected and in others totally disconnected, but I always had a general sense of displacement. It was as if I was a different color, and everyone but me could see this.

Even in my family, I felt like there was something missing. This was not because I had a bad childhood; as far as childhoods go, mine was quite excellent. My parents were wonderful—making mistakes of course, but always full of love and support.

The problem was not one of privilege or lack thereof, but rather one of spiritual emptiness. I had a hole in my heart, and nothing I encountered seemed to fix it. I felt like a stranger in the most familiar of circumstances, and even though I felt my family emanating the most unconditional love possible, there was still the very real fear that it was going to be snatched from me.

In time I sought to fill that hole in many of the usual ways. When I was about eight or nine I would attend church regularly and found some comfort there, but the church's view of the relationship between God and humans was so very conditional that it seemed to mimic the limitations I was already experiencing on an earthly level. During my teen years I tried to fill the hole with sex and drugs. Again, these were very temporary solutions. No matter what drug I used, I would eventually sober up. No matter how great the orgasm, I would still feel empty.

It was out of this intense searching that I had a profound realization. For all the wonders of this world, I did not belong here. I was a stranger in a very strange land, and I knew that my soul's purpose was, not unlike Dorothy's, to find my way home.

I thought I was unique, but in this, too, I was mistaken. As I began to walk my Yellow Brick Road, I started to meet others who could identify with my sense of "being lost" and I began to realize that it was indeed the cornerstone of the human condition. When we really look at what humans are feeling and experiencing, everyone is searching for a way to get back to "Kansas," and the great spiritual masters who have come out of every culture on earth have known this. In a wide variety of ways, they have shown us how to get there.

Some of us have close ties to our childhood home and others can move from home to home or from town to town on a whim. But on a spiritual level, we are homeless. The physical universe is a wonderful place to be, at least most of the time, but it is not our true home. We are spiritual beings having an experience that is physical, and when we lose sight of that, we feel a nagging emptiness and grief.

In the Oz story, Kansas represents home. It is the place where Dorothy feels safe and cared for—a place where she knows that the love of her Auntie is unconditional and readily available.

Various spiritual traditions have had names for Kansas. A Christian may refer to the "Kingdom of God", while the Jewish tradition refers to the "Promised Land." In Islam there is talk of a "Garden, with cool streams and beautiful maidens."[3] In Buddhism they are seeking Nirvana. Whatever a person or religion chooses to call this place, most spiritual seekers agree that there is something being sought and the greater truth about who we are is beyond the temporary and finite.

Somewhere in every soul there is a homing beacon, and when it is triggered, that person is consumed by an insatiable desire to find wholeness. A spiritual rebirth takes place and that person remembers, though faintly at first, a time when perfect and unconditional love was an

---

[3] According to the *Oxford Dictionary of World Religions,* edited by John Bowker.

inseparable part of his or her existence. When this happens, the journey out of Oz is a swift, though precarious adventure. We may wander off course from time to time but the end is certain.

When I first starting thinking about *The Wizard of Oz* as a metaphor for spirituality, I was a bit confused as to where Kansas fits in to the spiritual picture. Let's face it, it's not a big tourist destination. It is flat and rather boring. I decided to meditate on Kansas for awhile to see what would come to me. Like many of my meditations, this one was filled with distractions. The color and flair of my day-to-day life kept dragging me from my contemplations on Kansas. Then it hit me like a bolt of lightning! Because Kansas is not the most exciting place on earth, it is a perfect metaphor for our spiritual home.

From childhood onwards we are over-stimulated by the things of this world—fine food and drink, sensual pleasures and sexual gymnastics; they all grab for our attention. No matter what it is, most of us are quick to hand our attention over to the worldly pleasure. Many are distracted by the bright and the flashy. If you don't believe me, just ask any advertising consultant.

On the surface, it is easy to question why Dorothy was eager to leave the Technicolor splendor of Oz in favor of the black and white drab of Kansas, but Kansas had something that Oz could never offer Dorothy—family.

Kansas, while not the most exciting place, is filled with the things that feed our souls. These spiritual nutrients include interconnectedness, unconditionality, and support. It's not that we don't experience these things from time to time in this world, but when we are in the spiritual equivalent of Kansas, we will have them without limit or cessation.

Oz, like our earthly home, is filled with many uncertainties. Time and space are the prison bars that hold the mind hostage in Oz. We are doomed to experience cause and effect, and death and rebirth are like a recurring nightmare as long as we stay in Oz.

Oz and Kansas are two very different places. Oz is temporary; Kansas is eternal. Oz is an illusion; Kansas is our ultimate reality. Oz will dissolve into nothingness when we eventually wake up to find that we never left Kansas. Oz is full of paradox and contradictions; Kansas is entirely consistent. In Oz, all affection is based on conditions; in Kansas all affection is unconditional.

Recognizing that Oz is an illusion is not easy. Oz is like an ocean wave. It is part of the ocean, but it will pass and dissolve back into the ocean. It exists for a moment and then will be gone. The ocean, however, will last forever. This is why everything in the land of Oz will change, and everything in Kansas will be consistent.

Our journey out of Oz is nothing more than identifying ourselves with the ocean rather than the wave, with Kansas rather than Oz, with Spirit rather than the physical. Once we do this, the physical universe becomes our playground. We can mold it and shape it like play dough and then recreate it when we feel we need a change. The only way to do this, however, is to fully realize that the physical universe, Oz, is an expression of the creative aspect of God[4] working through us. It is not us. The Oz of our experience can be as beautiful or as ugly as we choose to make it, but the essential truth about it is that it is not our home and never will be. Once we realize this, we can return home at will. Until we realize this we will be orphans.

---

[4] I use the word God in the most general sense of the word. I do not view God as being male or female, or as belonging to any one religion. It is simply a word that describes the omnipresent, creative force of love that underlies all of creation.

# Munchkinland

*"The Munchkins will see you safely to the border of
Munchkinland. . ."*

—Glinda, *Good Witch of the North* (MGM)

Every journey must begin somewhere and ours begins in our childhood tribe. It is this childhood tribe that the Munchkins represent. They are our parents and our siblings, our teachers and our babysitters. They are sometimes related by blood, and other times wander into our lives by happenstance. They may be there by fate or perhaps just the luck of the draw, but they are there, and they will mold our lives, for better or for worse.

For some souls, such as Dorothy, the childhood tribe can be a very supportive environment. They greet the young soul with enthusiasm and celebrate her arrival. The soul is made to feel welcome and important. The value of the soul is never understated in this type of tribe, and her talents and skills are acknowledged.

Other souls are born into a tribe that is less than supportive. For whatever reason, the people who surround this soul do not have the eyes to see the gift that is before them. They see the soul more as a burden than a gift. They treat her with malice and disrespect, and in severe cases can be abusive.

Of course our lives are not so black and white. Most of us fall into tribes that are somewhere in between the above extremes. No humans are perfect and this includes parents and the others who surround a young soul. No humans are all evil either, so our experience is usually somewhere between the two poles.

Our childhood tribe has a few very important functions. First, they are there to lay out the ground rules. They teach us to chew with our mouths closed and to say our "please and thank you's." Placing a napkin in your lap is not going guarantee spiritual success, but the bits of advice that our childhood tribes offer us do make the time we spend in Oz a bit more smooth. Of course, not all tribes do the best job of preparing us for our journey through Oz. However, knowing the ground rules makes it that much easier for us to transcend the need for these rules later on in life.

The second function of the Munchkins is to teach us the tools and direction we need to find our way home. These tools may come in a religious context or a strong educational context, but in a healthy tribe they are offered as a means of liberation, rather than as a means to control and manipulate. It would be nice to think that our religious and educational institutions were all about supporting individuals in their quest for Kansas, but far too often that is not the case.

So many religions have become "houses of hatred,"[5] loading "heavy burdens"[6] upon people's backs. Rather than offering freedom, they have added more links to chains that bind. Education has largely become a system of programming, rather than an inspirational force to encourage free thought and creativity. This is a great tragedy. Rather than reminding us of our ruby slippers[7], these institutions have filled them with cement in an effort to prevent us from rocking the boat and challenging the status quo.

---

[5] From the song *Innocence Maintained* by Jewel on her CD *Spirit* (1999) Atlantic Recording Company.
[6] Matthew 23:4.
[7] The ruby slippers will be discussed in detail in Chapter Two.

The third and final goal of the tribe is to escort the soul to the edge of Munchkinland. They cannot make the journey for us, but having the support of our childhood tribe can really help. In far too many cases, tribes do not support their children in their spiritual journeys because it means saying goodbye, and it takes an exorbitant amount of faith that the young souls have learned their lessons well.

It has been said, *"To have a child, is to forever have your heart walk around outside your body."* I suspect this is a very true statement. The practice of surrender is one of the hardest spiritual principles in which to engage, but it is essential to the health of our children and the survival of our planet. Every soul has a purpose, and the job of the tribe is to give them the tools to get that job done. The job itself, however, must be taken on by the individual, and the tribe's biggest job is to let him or her do just that and not get in the way.

## The Emerald City

*"The Emerald City! [I'll] take you anyplace inside and show you the sights. . . first let me take you to a place where you can tidy up a bit."*

—The Wizard [disguised as the gate keeper] (MGM)

Leaving our childhood tribe is an essential part of our growth and evolution. For some of us this will involve a physical distancing, but that is in no way required. The leaving of our childhood tribe is more a coming into our own. It is the process of acquiring autonomy and redefining ourselves in our own way and in our own words. Once we do this we're ready to begin building our own tribe based on our own spiritual needs and goals.

There are several steps to building this new tribe, the first of which is acknowledging the "sins" of our childhood tribe. As I stated earlier, our parents are not perfect. No one is. Even the parents with the best of intentions make mistakes, and those mistakes become our first lessons. Whatever a parent or tribal member did to a soul, that soul must acknowledge it and move on to step two.

Step two is forgiveness. Without forgiveness we are doomed to recreate our childhood tribe with all its mistakes and misgivings. Many people think that just because they move far away or stop talking with their family, they are somehow free. The reality is they have not even begun to leave Munchkinland.

Forgiveness in its popular form is nothing more than a sugar-coated guilt trip. "You hurt me and you deserve to die, but I in my kindness will let you live." True forgiveness is about letting go of the past altogether and seeing God in that person. All beings are expressions of God, and nothing we do can change that. From the murderer on death row to the Peace Pilgrim,[8] God exists in all. Our forgiveness or lack of forgiveness will not change that fact. The main thing forgiveness does is free us up to live in the moment. It allows us to see our adult relationships in clear and untainted ways and it allows us to be replenished by them rather than held back. There is a saying: "Our parents are good at pushing our buttons because they are the ones who put them there." That may be true, but forgiving them is the only way to deactivate those buttons.

---

[8] From 1953 until 1981, the Peace Pilgrim (she renounced her birth name) walked back and forth across the United States with nothing but the clothes on her back, as a peaceful protest against violence. Her book, *Peace Pilgrim: Her Life and Work in Her Own Words,* is available through Blessingway Books.

When we forgive our parents we can stop dating them. They will no longer be our co-workers and our bosses. They will not be our friends and associates. We will stop encountering them around every corner. It's not that the behavior of the people in our lives will change—*we* will. We will stop seeking out people who embody the negative traits our parents had, and we will start being drawn to people who posses their positive qualities. We can form new and healthy relationships out of which our own children, should we choose to have any, can grow and evolve.

Once we forgive our childhood tribe, we can start to build the Emerald City in the physical world. The Emerald City is our chosen adult tribe. It is a support system that may or may not include members of our childhood tribe. While our childhood tribe is based on survival in the world, the Emerald City is based on spiritual evolution and growth. Its members will help, of course, with survival needs as they arise, but their primary focus is supporting us in our self-discovery, soul searching, and our return home.

I remember the first time I visited a yoga ashram[9] and spent time with some of the people who lived there. It was a profound experience. These people had all the same day-to-day problems the rest of us have, but they worked together to solve them. They approached life in a conscious way. They spoke truth to each other even when it was uncomfortable, and they expressed emotions freely without projecting them onto others.

What was most unique was the safety I felt. It was not that I had felt physically unsafe until that point, but that I was never asked for my thoughts and feelings. My crazy dreams were never embraced. Now, all of a sudden, large

---

[9] An ashram is a spiritual community much like a monastery.

groups of people were encouraging such things. It was like drinking water in the desert. I wanted to stay. In fact I had little desire to leave, but I knew in my heart I had to go. My place is in the world.

So I went back to my life, and one by one I began to meet others who were like me. My best friend Michael came into my life at that point and together we formed a meditation group. In time my circle of conscious friends grew, and my circle of semiconscious friends began to shrink. Today I am surrounded by conscious people. My friend David and I opened a Yoga studio that is the center of a growing community in the Castro District of San Francisco. Our goal is simply to provide a safe place for people to grow and evolve. Our neighbors have turned up in droves and they have slowly but surely become our family.

And so it goes on. People all over the place are deciding to let go of their past anger and bitterness. They are starting to forgive their childhood tribes and are building networks of friends that support them, love them, and want them to grow as spiritual beings. Men are allowed to cry; women are allowed to think. Ethnic minorities, gay men, lesbian women and religious minorities are beginning to co-mingle and our differences are fading into the background.

World peace will not arrive when there is no pain on the earth. World peace will come when we stand witness to the pain of our brothers and sisters, rather than trying to fix it or sleep through it. When we hold their hands and let them know they are not alone, then the seeds of world peace will be planted, and a global Emerald City will surely spring forth.

# Chapter Two

# Dorothy

Dorothy represents the soul—the part of each being that is beyond the limited physical earthly and temporal experience. It is the essence and the core of our being that is eternal, unchanging, and free. The soul is the "I" in "I am"[1] and it is the "Atman."[2] It has existed since before birth and will continue to exist after death. It is, like its creator, infinite.

Understanding the soul and acknowledging the power that it contains is a fundamental part of any spiritual journey. There is little progress that can be made in any spiritual pursuit until the value of the soul is recognized. Until then, the ego will surely have its way with us. Once we begin to recognize the true value and power of the human soul, there is little the ego can do to prevent our rapid return to Kansas.

---

[1] Exodus 3:14 & John 8:58.
[2] According to the Hindu and Sikh traditions, the Atman is the true self.

# The Ruby Slippers

*"Those slippers will never come off as long as you are alive."*
—The Wicked Witch of the West (MGM)

We are all born with a spiritual inheritance. It comes from God and it is given freely to all beings. This gift has immense power and can be used for good or for evil, or it can be loaned to others to use or misuse as they see fit.

In the Oz story this inheritance is symbolized by the ruby slippers. They are given to Dorothy at the start of her journey and they travel with her the whole way. It is not until the end that she learns how to use them, however.

Like Dorothy, each of us has a divine gift. We each carry within us the power to move mountains, but learning to use this power is a lifetime (or lifetimes) of work. It is not that the power is absent, but we must know where to look for it.

For most of us, that search begins with things that exist outside ourselves. We search in sex, prestige, food, money, relationships and work, but none of these things have any real or lasting power. The power of the ruby slippers is not of this world. Their full power is present with every soul, but for most it is largely unrealized. It exists merely as a potential rather than as a conscious reality.

The ruby slippers have three qualities that need to be realized if we are going to engage their power and use them to carry us home. First, they are given with free will attached. God did not give them to us with conditions. We can use them or not use them. They can be ignored or denied; they can be used for death or for life. God will not interfere.

Collectively and individually we have, to a limited degree, learned how to use our slippers. The whole process of evolution is the process of learning how to use them. Sometimes our heads and our hearts don't evolve at the same rate, however. Just because we know how to use something doesn't mean we are ready to handle the responsibility that comes with it.

The best example of this is in the splitting of the atom. It takes a huge amount of mental evolution to even discover that an atom exists, let alone split one in half. Talk about immense amounts of energy! Once that happened, humanity has been faced with the decision to live or die. We now have access to more power than people one hundred years ago would have thought possible. We have built bombs with this power.

Many ask why God would allow such things and the answer is free will. Real love must involve free will or it is not real love. There is a line in a song that says, "a bird in a cage will forget how to fly. . . if you love me, give me wings."[3]

The love of God is immense and unconditional. And because of that love there are no cages. We have been given the wings to fly in the gift of the ruby slippers. The question is, "When will we choose to use them?"

The next quality that our ruby slippers possess is their complete dominance over the laws of this world. Most of us operate our lives under the laws of cause and effect and within the parameters of time and space. These basic truths about our physical existence are so much a part of us, we doubt that miracles are possible.

When we start operating our lives with the power of

[3] From the song *Give Me Wings* by Michael Johnson from his CD *Then and Now* (released in 1997).

the slippers, we shift the rules. We start obeying the laws of a higher order, and then miracles are no longer doubted; they are a natural part of our day-to-day life. The laws of the physical universe still exist, but they bow to the divine laws that govern the ruby slippers.

Learning to use the ruby slippers is much like the evolution of modern physics. Isaac Newton identified such laws as gravity and the relation between mass and movement. These laws are still true today, but we now have, thanks to Albert Einstein, concepts such as relativity that are a higher law. The new laws don't negate the original laws. They just transcend them.

It is for this reason that we are able to move mountains and do even greater things[4] with our ruby slippers. It is for this reason that we will be carried home with neither time nor space presenting an obstacle. There is no order of difficulty in miracles.[5]

The third principle that governs the use of our slippers is faith. Having all the power in the universe, which we do, is of no use whatsoever if we don't have faith. It is through faith that the power of the slippers is activated. It is an essential ingredient.

The slippers are like the pilot light on a stove. The flame is always there inside waiting to ignite our lives, allowing us to burn away all obstacles to our peace. In order for this to happen, however, we need to turn up the gas. The gas is, of course, faith. The more faith we pump into our shoes, the faster and more effectively they will bring us home.

Faith is the most important ingredient in any healing, be it physical, emotional or psychological. It is faith that

---

[4] Matthew 17:20.
[5] From *A Course in Miracles*.

fuels our lives and allows the power of our spiritual inheritance to lift us to a higher law. It is faith, in combination with our divine inheritance, that allows our karma to be gently erased and our souls to rest.

## The Blue and White Dress

*"My dress is blue and white checked," said Dorothy, smoothing out the wrinkles in it.*

*"It is kind of you to wear that," said Boq[6].*
*"Blue is the colour of the Munchkins, and white is the witch colour: so we know you are a friendly witch."*

—Dorothy & Boq (Baum)

Although my book focuses on the MGM movie, I found this passage from Baum's book to be highly symbolic. While the movie doesn't touch on the colors of Dorothys outfit, the rich quality of the above statement is worth noting.

The Munchkins, as noted in Chapter One, represent our childhood tribe. The Good Witch represents Spirit. Dorothy's clothes, then, represent a blend of the physical with the spiritual. And it is this that she presents to the Land of Oz.

Many of us feel torn at times between our spiritual nature and our physical nature. It is as if there were two forces pulling us in different directions—one wanting us to survive in the world and the other wanting us to evolve— one that sees life in the short term and one that sees the bigger picture. My friend Sue often says that sometimes you can see the trees, and other times you can see the forest.

---

[6] In the book, *Boq* is one of the Munchkins.

Like Dorothy, we are cloaked in our humanity and our divinity. These two different aspects of our being are interwoven like the threads of Dorothy's dress. To let go of one means to let go of the other and to deny one means to deny the other. There is no way around this and yet both aspects of our being seem to be pulling us in different directions.

This, of course, creates a conflict within our soul that engenders guilt and fear. We seem to be faced with a choice. Survival in the here and now, or spiritual and moral stability. It is, on the surface anyway, a lose-lose proposition. We can see all too well what happens when we exploit one over the other.

Many are called to lead secular lives—these are the householders who have spouses and children and careers. Even those of us who don't desire a traditional tribe feel a calling to be part of a community and to give back to our society in some way—be that through art or music, or an improved social condition. While these are noble goals, there is a part of us that longs to express our spiritual side— to seek a deep and direct experience of the divine.

This deep divide in our psyche engenders a great deal of guilt. As a result, all sorts of religious abuse happens. People are funneled into church pews like livestock and told they are not good enough, and that they need some special brand of salvation to make their lives complete. If you want to create a best selling product, just look at some of the deep psychological needs that most of the people have and find a way to fill them. Opportunities for wealth and power have corrupted the religions.

Religious traditions do hold something or they would not be so profitable. Most religions play on people's fear and guilt, offering them just enough "God" to keep them spiritually alive, but never giving them enough tools to experience God first hand, allowing them to soar. Rather than being a platform from which to jump, most religious institutions have held the masses back.

However, there have been, and still are, people who seek something more. They are mystics and they come from every walk of life. Some mystics have been ordinary folk like Walt Whitman and William James. Others in both East and West have been ascetics, for in some religions a direct relationship with God was said to be impossible unless you were to give up the world and all its pleasures. The idea was simple: *Provide for your tribe and don't think for yourself.*

Asceticism meant renouncing the world, denying the desire for family and social interaction and devoting one's life entirely to spiritual pursuits. Living in a cloistered environment was commonplace. The tightly hidden mystical teachings of the various spiritual traditions were the reward for leaving the world behind.

There was no place for the ascetic in the world. Householders were encouraged to admire the ascetics[7] from afar, but the mainstream had no real desire to understand or invite the mystical traditions into day-to-day life, at least until recently.

An unprecedented thing has recently been happening on a global scale. Over the past twenty years or so people have been "leaving the church and finding God."[8] The churches and temples which the people are leaving are those rooted in past ways. The vast divide between the religion of the masses and the mystical traditions of the few is beginning to lessen. People, religious and secular, are beginning to explore prayer, meditation and other

---

[7] The terms "householder" and "ascetic" are Buddhist, but they describe a common dynamic in most cultures.
[8] *How to Talk Dirty and Influence People* by Lenny Bruce.

mystical practices such as Tai Chi, Yoga[9] and the Khabbala.[10] They are incorporating them into their day-to-day lives. More and more, people are beginning to define God in their own terms; terms that are based on their own personal experience with the Divine rather than rehashing the words and dogmas passed on to them by Popes and Rabbis, Gurus and Lamas.

Twenty years ago people would have laughed at you if you told them that doctors would be prescribing meditation and people would be praying in the operating room. You never would have been given sacred mantras to chant or been encouraged to engage in Christian centering prayer. While many Jews and philosophy majors may have heard of the Kabbalah, it was never practiced by a common Jew, let alone a gentile.[11]

Something amazing is happening in the world. People are returning to their spiritual center. They are learning to fully blend the blue and white fibers of their human experience. We are collectively changing the face of spiritual life on planet Earth. Caste systems are beginning to die, women are starting to have an equal role in many churches, and gay men and lesbian women are being accepted as spiritual beings. Long-standing dogmas are being questioned. Of course, it is a natural law that every action evokes a reaction.

This is a painful change in some ways. There are still many people who don't want things to change. The status quo serves a few people in power, though only on a superficial level at best. Getting people to feel good about themselves, and having them go directly to the source, cuts

---

[9] Yoga and Tai Chi are two forms of mysticism from the Eastern cultures that are growing in popularity here in the West.

[10] Kabbalah (or Qabbalah) is a form of Jewish mysticism that is becoming popular among Jews and non-Jews alike.

[11] Gentile is a word used by Jews to describe people who are non-Jews

out the middleman. Those middlemen are going to lose, so you can't expect them to go quietly.

The tides have already turned and the children of planet earth are looking mighty fine in their blue and white dresses! Someday, and I suspect it will be in my lifetime, things will look different. Our work and family life will be intrinsically woven into our spiritual life. Many will still visit churches, synagogues and temples, but not to hear lectures about what is right and wrong. Rather they will gather to celebrate a God that is as diverse as the people She created. There will be not one aspect—from sleeping to sex to eating and child rearing—that will not fully integrate the fibers of our blue and white dress. Life will become our spiritual practice.

## There's no place like home

*All I kept saying to everyone was, "I wanna go home." And they sent me home. .*

—*Dorothy (MGM)*

Dorothy had a mantra.[12] It was, "I want to go home", or some variation on that. No matter what her situation, she kept repeating this phrase over and over again. This was the prayer of her heart  the thing she desired above all else. It was this that got her through, and because of her determination and hard work, she did, in the end, get home.

As I mentioned earlier in the chapter, each soul is given a gift—the ruby slippers. This gift gives us immense power which is at our disposal even if we don't know how

---

[12] A mantra is a sacred word repeated over and over again as part of a meditation.

to use it. Anything we want is ours because of these shoes, but the trick is to really know what we want.

On the surface, we seem to be very clear about what we want. For most it would be material comfort, peace of mind, health, and wholesome, well-adjusted relationships. Yet, as we look at our lives, we may become aware of just how few of these things we actually have. And so it might be easy to dismiss the fact that we're even wearing shoes.

Here is the catch. We are given everything we ask for, but we have to ask from the deepest level of our being. We need to have our primary goal exposed and brought to light so that we can make a conscious decision about how to use our ruby slippers. This is true of our individual choices as well as our collective ones.

I once had a roommate who was looking for a husband. Her goal, or at least what she was conscious of, was to find a man who was nice, creative, attractive, and enjoyed all the romantic amenities, such as long walks on the beach, and most of all, had spiritual and emotional stability. This is not an unreasonable request. In fact they are standards that would serve most of us well when choosing a mate.

The interesting thing about this story is not what she thought she wanted, but what she chose for herself. Over the course of the year we lived together, she dated two men. The first was perfect by her own set of standards. He was a model, made a lot of money, was very charming, and loved quiet romantic things like long walks on the beach. She dumped him for bachelor number two who was jealous, moody, uptight, physically out of shape, and violent.

I am not about to excuse the behavior of her second fling; there is no excuse for not dealing with one's issues. Nor am I saying that the first guy was perfect in every way.

The thing that is odd is how a person (or group of people) can say one thing and manifest another.

Another example of this is the way that we, as a culture, can say that we want peace—that no child should go without food or medicine, and that a good education is invaluable. We really do believe this in much the same way a child believes in the Easter Bunny. But the reality is that we spend our money on weapons of destruction rather than on food, medicine and education.

This is where practices like meditation come in handy. They allow us to look at our deeper desire for things other than a return to Kansas. This is a difficult and painful process because it means acknowledging the fact that we choose all our unhealthy relationships, money problems, jobs we hate, and a society that puts death ahead of life.

This acknowledgment is difficult to be sure, but it is the first step in changing our deep desire for destruction to a deep desire for homecoming. Once this fundamental shift occurs, our souls can begin to say, "There is no place like home," and really mean it.

It's not that we will never get distracted by the tricks of the Wicked Witch, but they will not keep us captive for any real length of time. Things that once distracted us for days now get processed in hours, and things that threatened to overwhelm us before, now wash over us like a warm summer rain. Once our soul is again in charge, our journey home is swift, and no amount of smoke and mirrors from the ego will be able to make us forget who we are or where we are headed.

# Toto

*"Toto, I have a feeling we're not in Kansas anymore."*

—Dorothy (MGM)

There is a part of our soul that is wild and free—an aspect of our nature that is creative, off the wall and always looking for adventure. It seems to get us into trouble, but really this aspect of our soul is what leads us to our greatest lessons. It is this wild side that Toto represents.

Dorothy and Toto are inseparable through most of the story. In fact, there is only one brief scene in the witch's castle (where Toto runs for help), when they are apart.

Toto is unique as far as the Oz story goes, because he comes with Dorothy from Kansas, and he leaves with her at the end. The other figures may have existed in both lands, but they were there of their own accord. Toto is so deeply connected to Dorothy, that I have come to view him as an extension of her rather than his own separate entity.

Throughout the movie, Toto has one major function— to rock Dorothy's world. From the get-go when he bites Elmira Gulch, he is always getting Dorothy into a jam. On the surface, it might be easy to wonder why Toto is so important to Dorothy, but when you really think about it, he gives her life meaning by forcing her to look at life in new ways. He is the catalyst that brings her life's lessons to the surface, and then keeps them fresh in her mind until they are learned.

If it weren't for Toto, Dorothy never would have found the Land of Oz. She never would have challenged the Lion's cowardice, and would never have looked behind the curtain to see the truth about the Wizard. Even in the last scenes in Oz, it is Toto who jumps out of the balloon, knowing that Dorothy has not yet fully learned her lessons.

At first, it is not easy to trust the part of our soul that Toto represents, because on the surface he seems so irresponsible. There is not a lot of reason in the things he wants us to do, but he always leads us to a new adventure and a new lesson, which shapes who we are and brings us only that which is for our greater good.

One example of Toto working in my life happened recently while I was in Thailand with my friend Megan. We were on a small tropical island called Ko Phi Phi in the Andaman Sea. The island is very remote and has relatively few inhabitants. On one morning, I felt my spirit calling me off into the hills. I didn't know why or where I needed to go, but the pull was strong. Toto was barking!

Megan preferred to stay back at the bungalow and rest, so I took off for a hike alone. The views were magnificent when I reached the top of the island, but it was not until I began my hike down the other side that I realized what Toto had in store for me.

As I meandered through the thick rain forest, I came to a small clearing filled with thousands of butterflies. It was the most enchanting thing I had ever seen. I was stopped dead in my tracks and closed my eyes. There were so many butterflies that I could feel the gentle brush of air on my face that the hundreds of tiny wings were creating. There was nothing but silence and I had the opportunity to experience this beautiful moment—one that could never have been created out of responsibility or logic.

For many, going on an "irresponsible adventure" is not in their nature, and they would prefer to play it safe. They try to get a guarantee out of life, but none exists. In the end the depressing realization that life has been a boring waste of time is sure to accompany the "safe" path that so many try to follow. Following Toto is the only way to really taste the spice of life. Toto is the part of our soul that makes our lives salty[1], and keeps us humble.

If you keep a dog locked away in your house, it should not surprise you when he craps all over your floor. Likewise when we keep Toto locked behind the prison bars of false security and "responsible behavior," our lives will reek of death as we rot from the inside out.

Letting Toto out to run wild is scary. He is a part of us, and when we let him out, it is natural to fear he will run away. But the only thing Toto exhibits in the movie, to a greater extent than his insatiable sense of adventure, is loyalty.

His adventure is not about acting foolishly. His adventure is about trusting the wisdom of the soul. He is loyal to Dorothy and to what is for her own good, yet he doesn't feel the need to explain himself. He sees a curtain and pulls it back. He sees a cat and he jumps to play. He is not careless at all, just spontaneous. If it feels right to him, he doesn't stop to question. He acts on a deep instinct rather than taking the time to get it all in his head.

His loyalty and his spontaneity are qualities that we would all do well to cultivate to the fullest, because in many ways he is the most important figure in the whole story. When we choose to keep the Toto part of our soul on a short leash, we do limit our lives. This may or may not succeed in bringing us the illusion of security, but it will never bring us fulfillment.

---

[10] Matthew 5:13.

Evolution only happens when we step outside of the comfortable and the known. People who really change the world are the ones who seek a new way of looking at things and then go beyond what is familiar. In short, people who evolve personally, and in turn help their communities to evolve, are the ones who have the courage to let Toto off his leash and trust him enough to follow where he leads.

# Chapter Three

# Glinda the Good Witch of the North

*"Look, here is someone who can help you."*

—Scarecrow (MGM)

The Good Witch of the North represents the spirit of guidance that leads the soul along its journey. She is the principle in nature that inspires trees to blossom in the spring and reminds birds that it is time to fly south in the winter. She is the force present in our own bodies that heals broken bones and regulates the cycles of growth, maturity and reproduction.

It is easy to ignore her and even easier to take her for granted, but she is ever present. We can deny, desecrate and defame her, but she will not go away.

For many years, the common religious belief was that Spirit and nature were somehow separate, but mystics and shamans have known this to be a great falsehood. The same

Spirit that tells a mustard seed to grow into a great tree[1] is the same Spirit that can navigate our lives, steering us around the many pitfalls we may encounter along our spiritual journey.

Many people combine the words, "soul" and "spirit," seeing them as synonymous, but doing this blurs some very important truths. While the spirit is an inseparable part of the soul, it is also the part of us that knows truth. It is the part of us called by some the higher mind, the Buddha Nature, or the Christ Mind. It is the element of our soul that sees through illusion—the aspect of our nature that knows of Oz, but also knows how to guide us along our journey toward Kansas.

The beautiful thing about the Good Witch is that she is always there when Dorothy most needs her, though Dorothy is rarely aware of it. She inspires Dorothy in subtle ways and gently wakes her from her dream of Oz. She is there at the beginning to greet Dorothy, and she is there at the end to see her off. In a sense she never left Dorothy's side.

## Good Witches and Bad Witches

*"And so, what the Munchkins want to know is, are you a good witch or a bad witch?"*

—Glinda (MGM)

The symbolism in the question, "Are you a good witch or a bad witch?" is quite rich and embodies the crux of spiritual evolution. It represents the very question the Spirit asks the

---

[1] Mark 4:30-32.

soul every moment of every day. It is the same as asking us to choose the path we will walk, the master we will serve[2] and the voice to which we will listen.[3]

Before we can understand the differences between a good witch and a bad witch, I think it is important to understand what a witch is. When we strip away myth and legend, fear and misconception, we find something rather interesting about witchcraft. Witchcraft is a very old, very beautiful religion which centers itself around the cycles of nature and our interconnectedness with the earth. It also teaches that we are co-creators with the Divine. It is this co-creating or "spell casting" that is at the heart of Glinda's question.

In a sense, we are all witches because we are all co-creating with the Divine all the time. Whether we are consciously aware of it or not, we are continuously casting spells and shaping the world with our thoughts, beliefs and actions. When we co-create as a good witch, we heal the planet and propel humanity along its evolutionary journey. When we co-create as a bad witch, we conquer and destroy, we deepen our own sleep, and we encourage others to remain unconscious too.

The vast majority of the people do not realize their co-creative ability and thus hand their co-creative birthright over to others. World War II is one such example of this. Hitler was clearly serving the "bad" witch. His self serving ego-driven behavior was a clear statement of his choice to use his co-creative power to darken the world. In fact, he served the Wicked Witch so well that he himself has become an archetype synonymous with hers.

While Hitler was responsible for the deaths of countless people, he does not share that burden alone. He may have

---

[2] Luke 16:13.
[3] *A Course in Miracles.*

been a charismatic leader hell-bent on serving the ego, but there were thousands of people who quickly denied their ruby slippers and exchanged them for a good economy and a false sense of nationalism.

The Europeans who followed Hitler were not bad people, any more than the Americans who have done nothing to end persecution and bigotry in the United States. While most of us are not involved in sins of commission, there are few of us who have not committed sins of omission. Hitlers, Stalins and David Dukes are bound to show up once in a while, but their ability to cause trouble is significantly reduced when the masses refuse to turn their heads in fear.

To listen to the voice of the Good Witch is to use our co-creative powers with the Divine for our own growth and the evolution of our planet. It means much more than living a moral life, meaning to do no harm, though that is an important first step. The Good Witch blesses the world with her words, thoughts and deeds. She seeks to return home, but she also realizes that the only way to do this is to walk consciously and honorably.

She treats the small stuff with the same reverence and attention as she does the big stuff. While her commitment is unshakable, her ability to smile at herself and be flexible is undeniable. She is both strong and gentle, civil and wild, creative and receptive. She speaks the truth, which is the potent medicine she uses to heal the world; and while that medicine may be a difficult pill to swallow, she always offers it with nurturance and kindness.

On an emotional level the Good Witch feels pain as well as pleasure, but she is driven by neither. Whether she is sitting in a house of tears or a house of laughter, she knows joy because both houses are built on foundations of faith, perseverance, and a deep connection with the Divine.

The path of the Good Witch is not always easy, but it is always inspired, guided and full of purpose. Everything she does is a lesson for herself and for the world. She draws strength from her inner wisdom, but she views the world with the newness and purity of a child's eyes. She lives as a maiden and a knight, a mother and a father, an old sage and a medicine woman.

To listen to the voice of the Bad Witch on the other hand is quite different. The Bad Witch is motivated by fear and uses her co-creative powers, consciously or unconsciously, to gain pleasure and to avoid pain. She forms relationships, but only when they serve her. When possible, she is present and "loving," but make no mistake about it, her "love" is very conditional and will be turned to rage if you challenge her perception of reality.

She denies her dark side by pointing out the faults and failures of others, using their different beliefs, behavior and appearance as an excuse to hate. She reacts based on her perceptions of the past rather than acting from her inner wisdom in the present moment, and she misuses her co-creative power in order to form the future in the dark image of the past, thus making sure that history will indeed repeat itself.

The Bad Witch may be an immoral person, or she may adhere to an ego-driven sense of morality that is strict and rigid, enabling her to declare that she "loves the sinner but hates the sin." Perhaps the most distinguishing difference between the moral code of the Good Witch and that of the Bad Witch is that the morality of the Good Witch is in place to ensure freedom, and the morality of the Bad Witch is in place to ensure imprisonment.

The Bad Witch cries out of her loneliness and laughs out of insecurity. This laughter is most times at the expense of others and is often a reflection of her dark side. Emotions to her are something to be feared and exploited, but never embraced.

It is tempting to think that an individual is all Good Witch or all Bad Witch, but the reality is that both are existing all the time in our unconscious. They live in a constant tug of war, fighting to see which one will rule our lives.

With every decision made, there is metaphorically a little devil sitting on one shoulder, screaming at the top of his lungs, "Look out for yourself. There is so much to be fearful of. Be on your guard or you will be crushed." On the other shoulder there is a small angel who gently whispers, "You are a perfect expression of the Divine. Your true Self is eternal and cannot be harmed or destroyed. Though my words may seem insane, if you decide with honor and courage, you will know the meaning of Joy."

When you choose to listen to the whisper of the tiny angel, you are living as a good witch. When you choose to listen to the screeching of the little devil, you are living as a bad witch. With this awareness, only one question remains. "Are you a good witch or a bad witch?"

## The Kiss of the Good Witch

*". . . I will give you my kiss, and no one will dare injure a person who has been kissed by the Witch of the North." (Baum)*

When Dorothy first arrives in Munchkinland, Glinda kisses Dorothy on the forehead—a seeming gesture of love, or possibly a quiet blessing. The book goes into a bit more detail than the movie. In the book the kiss comes at the point when Dorothy is ready to begin her journey on the yellow brick road.

*"Won't you go with me?" pleaded the little girl, who had begun to look upon the little old woman as her only friend.*

*"No, I can't do that," she replied, "but I will give you my kiss and no one will dare injure a person who has been kissed by the good Witch of the North."*

*She came close to Dorothy and kissed her gently on the forehead. Where her lips touched the girl they left a round shining mark. . ."*[4]

To be kissed by the Good Witch is one of the great gifts of the Spirit. It is a covenant[5] made between the soul and the creator. It is the guarantee that we will all find our way home. It is the commitment on the part of the Spirit that promises to always meet us where we are and guide us in whatever way we are best able to accept. The degree to which we are able to accept this gift is the degree that we will be able to experience serenity.

Various spiritual traditions have rituals such as baby blessings and baptisms to commemorate and remind us of this kiss. And while they are a nice sentiment, they are nothing more than that, for Glinda's kiss rests on all of us. Somewhere deep inside, there is a part of each individual that is wise and all-knowing—in complete attunement with the rest of the universe. This kiss lets it be known that it no longer matters how many drugs a person takes, how many sexual partners they have had, or how many times they have cheated, lied or stolen. It matters not what our grade point average is or how much money we give to the poor. It doesn't make any difference how many times you chant your mantra, receive consecrated bread, or fast. The kiss of the Good Witch, the mark of the Spirit, is universal and unconditional. It is our birthright, and like the inheritance

---

[4] *The Wonderful Wizard of Oz* by L. Frank Baum.
[5] Exodus 24:8.

of the prodigal son[6] it is waiting for us any time we choose to accept it.

With this kiss, we are guaranteed to find our way to Kansas. Why? Because this kiss holds the truth that we never left. So the question that naturally follows is: "Why do good deeds at all? Why not do whatever the hell I want, stepping on whomever I need to get my way? There is nothing to lose, for I have this guarantee, and I am going to milk it for all it's worth."

There is a simple answer. Just because we have a guarantee of success, doesn't mean the yellow brick road is not going to be long and hard. It also doesn't mean instant success or that we won't take long and painful detours into dark and fearful places. One of the great problems with most moral codes is that they are imposed with the threat of some form of outside punishment. The fear of eternal damnation or the belief that one will return in the next lifetime as an outhouse maggot are very poor reasons to abstain from doing anything, and as the nightly news will attest, their effectiveness is very questionable.

There is a famous saying that sums up this idea quite well. "We are not punished for our sins, but rather by our sins." In other words, we have complete freedom to do whatever we want. It is not a vengeful god that will keep us out of heaven, or a principle such as karma that will keep us from waking up. Oz is a dream from which we will all wake up, but how we choose to live our lives, the standards and values which we choose to abandon or embrace, and the quality of our actions, will be the deciding factor in whether we experience Oz as a nightmare or a quiet dream of peace.

Glinda's kiss leaves a mark on each of us that can not be washed off or erased. It is there for us to embrace or

---

[6] Luke 15:11-32.

deny, to share with the world or hide under a "bushel basket"[7] of fear. When we learn to see this mark in ourselves, we are magically able to see this mark in others, and when we deny this mark in ourselves, we are unable to experience it in others. At best we will live in codependence rather than interdependence. At worst we will wage war, globally, nationally and internally.

If you can imagine a world where we see people as spiritual beings rather than as having a race, religion, nationality or sexual identity, then you will have a very good idea of how the world will look when we are encouraged to show the mark of the Good Witch rather than the collective baggage of our past. In that image you will also see through the "mistakes" of others as well as your own, and growth and evolution will happen without effort, resistance and pain.

Recognizing this mark is, for most of us, very challenging. The gentle kiss of the Good Witch offers us so much, but it is so easy to forget. Let's face it. The dramatic entry of the Wicked Witch, complete with glass breaking laughter, smoke and fire, scares us so deeply that Glinda's gentleness retreats into the background of our minds.

The fear of the Wicked Witch colors our perception of Oz, so it is no wonder we view so many people as the enemy. Each person we meet is seen not as bearing the mark of the Good Witch, but rather as reminding us of our fear. "Self-defense" seems like a logical alternative. And far too often, we see offense as the best defense, thus perpetuating fear.

Through spiritual practices such as meditation and prayer in their many forms, we begin to recognize this mark of peace. We begin to transcend the ego, and we begin to see through the "special effects" of the Wicked Witch.

---

[7] Matthew 5:15.

As we begin to recognize this mark, we see it in all our brothers and sisters. We begin to see it in nature and art, in music and science. The "kiss of the Witch of the North" is as omnipresent as Spirit itself. As this transcendence continues, the illusion of Oz transforms itself from a dream of terror to a dream of peace, creativity, and joy. When this happens we can spend less time rearranging the furniture in our respective burning houses[8] and more time walking along our individual yellow brick roads toward the reality of Nirvana, the reality of Heaven, the reality of Kansas.

## Come out Come out

> *"She brings you good news or haven't you heard?*
> *When she fell from the sky, a miracle occurred."*
>
> —Glinda (MGM)

As I mentioned in chapter one, the Munchkins represent our childhood tribe. When Dorothy's house drops in Munchkinland, she frees them by destroying the Wicked Witch of the East. Glinda is called in by the Munchkins to help figure out the whole situation. This is very symbolic of evolution.

There is certainly no doubt that our tribes, both childhood and adult, help to shape the course of our lives. We are, to a greater or lesser degree, a product of our environments. This is one of the reasons we often feel a victim of the world, but when we shift our awareness from that of victim to co-creator, we become teachers and healers rather than victims; this is the real miracle.

---

[8] There is a famous Buddhist analogy about rearranging the furniture in a burning house, rather than helping people to escape to safety via spiritual practice.

Many people spend a great deal of time complaining about the government, their parents, and the sorry state of affairs in the world, but in doing so they forget that *we* are the miracle. They blame God for the suffering that surrounds us saying, "How could a loving God allow such things to happen?" They behave like slaves who blame an overseer, forgetting that free will has given them the responsibility, so that the deeper issue has nothing do with God or the government but rather with the fundamental shift that must occur in the human heart if peace is to become a reality. We think of responsibility as a burdensome obligation when in fact it is a gift.

When a child is born, new hope and new freedom are infused into the tribe. In most cases people smile with the hope that that child will make the world a better place. And indeed they have every reason to smile, for within every child is the potential for an enlightened society.

How we greet that child and how we treat her as she gets accustomed to the world can be decisive for the time when that soul presents her gift, the tiny seed that sparks a new level in our evolution. Understanding this, we may wonder how we have evolved as far as we have.

It is time we face the painful reality that we have given children the short end of the stick. As a result we are not experiencing the spiritual evolution of our culture and of humanity as a whole, but rather a devolution into gang wars, rampant drug abuse, and junior high school shootouts. The way we treat our children is a dreadfully scary reflection of our unwillingness to accept healing and our complete ignorance of the miracle that is before us.

In order to accept this miracle, we must come out of our spiritual closets and do three things. First, we need to acknowledge that a miracle is desperately needed. Until we do this, we are passengers on a sinking Titanic, listening to the music and dancing in our makeshift life vests. Just as human arrogance sank the Titanic, so our belief in a magic pill or a new technology to cure all ills will be our destruction. Until we do our emotional and spiritual homework, all the intellectual advances in the world are not going to save our collective butts. Doing this homework means acknowledging we have a problem, and recognizing that the solution is a spiritual one.

Second, we need to acknowledge that children are not just our best hope for the future, but our only hope. Until we lift up our children and make their spiritual, emotional, and physical well-being our priority, we are destined for a future that will make World War II look like a picnic. Imagine how different Dorothy's adventure would have been had the Munchkins greeted her with the same apathy as we greet our children. I can almost hear the Munchkin Mayor saying, "Sorry Dorothy, we don't have time to celebrate your arrival. We need to get back to work. There is so much to do. You just sit and become a mindless drone watching violent TV and playing video games. And for God's sake, don't get into any trouble or we will throw you into a juvenile detention center."

For parents, protecting the gift which children have to offer is obviously their job, though an alarming number of parents seem to have missed this point. Parenting is not the only way we must seek to create a world in which our children will flourish, however. We must learn to treat all children like human beings; we must remember that the Earth will be home to them deeper into the future than it will be for most of us; and we must work hard to break through our own patterns of disease, neurosis and spiritual dysfunction, lest we dump them in their laps.

The ways in which we break through these patterns are countless. For some it will be in the form of a twelve-step program, while others will find liberation in prayer, meditation and other mindful activities. One thing is for sure though—unless we deal with our own stuff, our children will have to; and the more we load upon their shoulders, the more difficult it will be for humanity as a whole to evolve and prosper.

The third thing we need to recognize is that there is no age at which we lose our ability to be miracle workers. About the time we get potty trained, we are methodically instructed to shut down. Conformity is praised and creativity is squelched. We are told that life is hard and we have to fight to get by. At first we rebel by tearing off our clothes in the supermarket and laughing in church, but eventually even the most free-spirited children will become "adults". Now I'm not suggesting that jumping in the fountain naked[9] is the best way to find enlightenment, but it might be a major step in our journey. Until we become like little children[10], we are not going to find Kansas. We need to sing and dance along our yellow brick road. We need to stop suffocating our "inner children" with psychobabble, and simply let them out to run wild. After all, what could be more spiritual than giggling in church?

Many truly believe they are free and that they are living as children because of our cultural obsession with youth; but if you think about it, there is a well-defined line between living as a child and living as a self-perpetuator If you were to take a child to the gym, force him to lift weights until he could no longer reach his toes, then pump him full of mind-altering drugs (doctor prescribed or otherwise), and then have his face and body surgically altered, you

---

[9] St. Francis is said to have ripped off his clothes and jumped in the fountain in the center of town when he renounced the world and began his spiritual life. This is reminiscent of the Gospel of Thomas, Logion 37: "When you disrobe without being ashamed...you will see the Son of the Living One."
[10] Mark 18:13.

would be thrown in jail for child abuse. But when we do this type of thing to ourselves, we call it self-improvement. Wow, are we in denial or what?

We eat produce laced with bug spray and animal products filled with steroids. American staples have become canned food, white bread, caffeine and Prozac. Exercise is done to excess or not at all, and job and family stress find their expression in road rage and domestic violence. We then wonder why cancer is on the rise, by-pass surgery is as common as a root canal, and women over forty need hormone therapy.

It is so essential that we look at these things directly and honestly if we are to work miracles in this suffering world. We are the same souls who fell from a star,[11] bringing so much promise to the world. Nothing but our perception of ourselves has changed. As we begin to realize this, we can take the next step—coming out.

After we have accomplished the above three tasks, we need to step boldly forward with faith and confidence. We need to listen to the voice of our Spirit singing, "Come out, come out wherever you are." You see, coming out is not just for gay men and lesbian women. It is not just about sexuality. It is about stepping out of our hiding and presenting ourselves as who we are called to be. This can be the most ominous and terrifying element in our spiritual process, but the freedom it brings with it is immeasurable.

We hide in jobs we hate, in marriages that don't satisfy us, and in addictions that threaten to destroy us. The number of closets we can hide in are countless. We pretend to have it all figured out, lest the neighbors discover that we struggle and experience fear, anxiety and rage. In a nutshell, we settle for lies, and what is worse, we are not

---

[11] From a song by Glinda, Good Witch of the North (MGM).

kidding anyone, least of all ourselves. These closets have become home. The only locks on our closet doors are the ones we believe are there, and by changing our minds, we are freed.

There is one very simple way to tell if you are living in a closet. Ask yourself, "Am I experiencing joy in this moment?" If the answer is "No", then you can be sure you are in a closet. This is not to say that life outside the closet is pain free, but the winds of pain and pleasure will no longer overwhelm you when they rattle your closet door. Instead you can learn to sail!

Leaving the closet means entering the battlefield of life[12], walking headfirst into our fears, and transcending them. This is where the miracle occurs. This is where wicked witches are laid to rest, and the true power of the ruby slippers is realized. This freedom is won not just for us, but for all in our tribes.

---

[12] In the Bhagavad Gita, Krishna instructs his student Arjuna to enter into "battle".

# Chapter 4

# The Wicked Witch of the West

## The Witch and the Ego

*"I'm afraid you've made rather a bad enemy
of the Wicked Witch of the West."*

—Glinda (MGM)

There are few spiritual concepts that are more elusive and difficult to understand than the ego. This is largely because everything we experience gets filtered through the ego, clouding our perceptions of it. Every time we try to analyze the ego, we get a slanted view. It is for this reason that metaphor is such a great tool. It allows us to sneak truth past the ego's defense system, stealth style, allowing us to "hear without hearing."[1] The Wicked Witch is one very apt metaphor for the ego.

---

[1] Matthew 13:13.

The Wicked Witch represents the part of the mind that believes it is separate from the rest of the mind and the rest of creation. It sees itself as existing in a vacuum, free from the "hassles" of interdependence. It fails to realize that this separation is impossible and that its belief in separation causes great pain. The Wicked Witch has taken a part of our mind hostage and made it her kingdom, and in order to cross from the Land of Oz to the Land of Kansas, we are required to go to the heart of her kingdom.

The Wicked Witch defines herself by such external things as gender, occupation, tribal affiliation and the like. She may or may not believe in God, but she always sees herself as separate from God. Guilt is her motivator and fear is her greatest weapon. She exists solely because of an individual's fear and guilt, so she stops at nothing to perpetuate them both.

We fear her and we respect her. We even have a love/hate relationship with her. Not unlike the movie, she makes our lives interesting. As a child, watching the movie every spring, I would nearly soil my pajamas when she would shriek across the screen. I hated her, but she gave me a tantalizing rush. To a certain degree, the Wicked Witch that is my ego still gives me that rush today.

There is a big part of me that loves her games and is thrilled by the drama she creates in my life. It was hard for me to admit this. Every relationship I found myself in was full of drama, and most of that drama was the cornerstone on which that relationship was built. When I was in high school my father and I would sit every Saturday morning and argue about current events. Not only did it drive the rest of my family nuts, but also it kept my father and I from having a meaningful conversation. This is a perfect scenario for the Wicked Witch in my head.

It is this rush that makes transcending the ego so

difficult. She has us believing that if we didn't play her game there would be nothing, but the reality is that without her we would experience everything. She knows this, and she will go to any lengths to get us to deny and betray our ruby slippers.

## Keeping Tight Inside Your Shoes

*"Keep tight inside of them. Their magic must be very powerful, or she wouldn't want them back so badly."*

—Glinda (MGM)

Keeping tight inside our shoes means not letting go of our principles. It means having our goal in sight and not taking our eyes off it. It means keeping our spiritual integrity intact even in the face of death. It means feeling fear and experiencing temptation and not bowing to them.

Keeping tight in our shoes is largely like the first commandment of Moses: "You shall put no other God before me." On a simplistic level, this means, don't build bronze statues and worship other "gods," but on a deeper, mystical level, it offers us an anchor with which to ground ourselves and our lives. It helps us to cut through the distractions that the Wicked Witch puts in our paths and it keeps our focus on the job at hand   liberation.

As a child I saw God as being petty and jealous. "He" would be angry if I paid attention to some other god and would punish me for not honoring him completely. Now my views have changed. I have to believe that God is at least as compassionate as humanity's most compassionate act and at least as logical as humanity's greatest intellectual achievements. In fact I would have to believe that "He" is all that and then some. To think that God is as petty and frail as some of humanity's darkest chapters is depressing and short-sighted, as it offers the believer nothing but guilt and fear.

With regard to the first commandment, the higher road is to realize that it is not a wrathful god that will punish us, but rather an ego gone crazy. To put anything between God and the soul is to set the individual up for disappointment, pain and despair. Nothing in this world will last. Empires will fall, mountains will be flattened. Our bodies will age, wither and die. If we worship any of these things we will absolutely feel pain, because they will never love us back and they will change. It is a fact that we must accept. Life in the physical means change, and it is only our attachment to the form of things that keeps us in bondage.

The Wicked Witch will entice us with sex, romance, wealth, power and every pleasure imaginable. None will bring us happiness, because even when we have them, we know on some level that they will not last. When we hold on to things we know will change, there is a base level of fear that permeates our existence even if we won't admit it to ourselves on a conscious level. Every orgasm will be followed by arousal, every drunken bout will be followed by the sobering reality of the pain we were trying to hide, and every relationship will have its painful moments. Money will come and money will go. All things in this world will change.

Keeping tight inside our shoes means doing our best not to worship these false gods. It means putting our spiritual life first in all things. Yes, even before our families, friends and lovers. Before our jobs, money and social status. Even before our religions, dogmas and beliefs. In the end, we need to fall back on the faith that we are powerful spiritual beings who will exist long after our bodies cease to be and our bank accounts are divided up by relatives and creditors.

Life can be hard and scary at times, but all fear and pain are caused solely by the belief that things in this world can bring us peace. It is the attachment to things that causes suffering. It is the letting go of these attachments that guides us safely along our path, helping us to realize the power of our shoes, and eventually it brings us home.

## The Field of Poppies

*"Now my beauty, something with poison in it, I think, with poison in it but attractive to the eye and soothing to the smell. . . Poppies will put them to sleep."*

—The Wicked Witch of the West (MGM)

We can choose to abandon our false idols at any time, but once we have involved ourselves with them, it becomes more difficult to let them go. The ego knows when something is a good piece of bait and will use any "addiction" to put us to sleep. Like an addiction to heroin, anything from TV to masturbation can lead us off track. Don't get me wrong, TV has the potential to be a wonderful medium, and masturbation has provided me with some of the best sex I have ever had, but when things such as these become compulsive, the ego will take you for a ride.

Being mindful of our compulsions and keeping them in check is one of the key ways to keep tight in our shoes. For me, there is no such thing as moderation when it comes to nicotine. I have friends who have a cigarette now and then and do fine. I am not like them. I was a three-pack-a-day smoker and I don't doubt that I would be again if I took even one puff. On a very deep level I believed that cigarettes were my best friend. They were there when I was hungry and there when I was full. They were there after sex and there when I was horny. They were there when I was sad and there when I was happy. If I only had a few dollars in my pocket, I would have chosen a pack of smokes over food. They came before all else, and they most certainly came before my spiritual life.

As we all know, smoking doesn't solve any problems, big or small. Cigarettes give us a temporary sense of reprieve at best, but in the long run they fail us. In many cases they do more than fail us; they destroy our health, deaden our senses, and create problems far bigger than the ones that we were trying to avoid. They are, for many, poppies that induce sleep and prevent entrance to the Emerald City.

Cigarettes are just one example. The obvious others are drugs, alcohol and food, but the list is endless. We have merely to look around at the things that people do mindlessly to see that the ego can turn almost everything into a poppy. Shopping, work, Internet chat rooms and television are a bit less obvious, but just as insidious.

The only way to get these addictions under control is to withdraw from them altogether. If you give your Wicked Witch an inch, she will have you. Getting the ego under control is a lot like training a puppy. Like a puppy, the ego wants your attention. It may do quiet and gentle things like licking your face, or it may crap all over your floor. Either way, the ego demands that you pay attention to it at all times. Should you begin training your ego, it will resist in much the same way a puppy might, but in time it will learn that a firm boundary has been set and that there is no room for negotiation in those areas.

Now if, while you are training a puppy, you give it

mixed signals by not being consistent in your commands, you will never train it in anything. For example, if you are trying to teach the puppy not to beg at the table, and you even once give in and offer a scrap of food, that puppy will never give up. It will remember the one time you gave in, rather than the hundred or so times that you didn't.

The field of poppies scene can teach us a lot in regard to our own addictions. First, just because the body and soul might be taking a nap doesn't mean our brain and our heart have checked out as well. Like the Oz story, we often realize that we are being "drugged" and we feel heartache over it, but that doesn't seem to be enough to pull us out. Ultimately, it is our Spirit that needs to pull us back to our path. How many of us can really argue with the idea that too much TV is not healthy? Or that smoking is unhealthy? Even people steeped in addiction would agree. Addiction is not a mental problem or a physical dependency. It's spiritual in nature and its solution must be spiritual as well.

Falling asleep in our own personal field of poppies is not something that most of us are really in denial about. Sure, for a time it is comforting to say that it is not a problem and that it is no big deal, but in our brain and in our heart, we know that we are deadening ourselves.

The solution is a spiritual one. Just as it took the blessing of the Good Witch to pull Dorothy out of her sleep, it takes the blessing of our Spirit to wake us from our addiction. But like Dorothy, both our brain and our heart need to ask for help first. Inviting the Spirit to heal us is the same as becoming willing in the Twelve Steps. We become like Abraham offering his son Isaac up to God[2]—trusting that in letting go of what we most cherish we will find transcendence, liberation and a direct experience of the divine.

---

[2] Genesis 22: 1-19.

Like Abraham, we are not asked to sacrifice anything, though it may appear that way initially. The only things Spirit asks us to give up are our pain, ignorance, fear and suffering. All other things are restored and renewed as the Spirit wakes us gently from the spell of the poppies.

## Insects and Monkeys

*"So they want my broom, eh? Well, they'll need a mop to clean up what's left of them after I'm done!"*

—Wicked Witch of the West (MGM)

As we have already discussed, the Wicked Witch is a part of the mind. She does not exist outside and therefore has no power to affect our external lives unless we give her that power. The darkness we experience in the world is but a shadow of the darkness that exists in our individual and collective minds. This darkness needs to be maintained and guarded by the Witch, or the immense power that our Spirit emanates would dispel her darkness without effort or consequence. For this reason the Wicked Witch has gathered together an army that wages a war inside our heads. They are the demons that keep us either paralyzed with fear or running for our lives. She uses these things to ensure our obedience and, when possible, to conquer new territory.

This army is represented by the Winged Monkeys, the Winkies[3] and the mysterious "insects." Each represents a different line of her defense system. It is these three things that we need to confront before we can really dissolve the belief system that is represented by the Witch herself.

The Insects don't have a huge part in the movie, and

---

[3] The Winkies were not mentioned by name in the movie.

don't exist at all in the book. In fact, if I had not watched the film a handful of times in preparation for this book, I would likely have missed the reference. During the scene where the Witch sends out the Winged Monkeys to retrieve Dorothy, she says, ". . . send the little insects on ahead to take the fight out of them!"[4]

The Insects represent the day-to-day concerns that plague our mind and keep us distracted. Paying the rent, contending with bills, fears about retirement and wondering just how the children will find their way through college, all drain our energy and take the fight out of us. These concerns seem so real and basic to our survival that it is rare that the Witch ever needs to move beyond this most basic platoon.

In the movie *Out on a Limb* which documents Shirley MacLaine's spiritual awakening, she's talking with a friend about her feeling that there's something missing. Frustrated, her friend says, "What could possibly be missing? Tell the man who drives the Wonder Bread truck, with four kids to feed, that you haven't got it all." Shirley tries to explain that it's not fame, money or success she's referring to, but a vague sense that there's something more to life. She says, "There's got to be more—maybe I realized it *because* I have so much."

The Insects don't take us down in one big hit, but rather through a series of little hits that keep us distracted from the spiritual issues that underlie our suffering and keep us in ignorance. Luckily we do have some spiritual bug spray that works quite well in neutralizing their ability to sting. It is faith. The development of faith that we mentioned in chapter two in connection with the ruby slippers is quite effective in keeping the Insects at bay and allowing us to move forward.

---

[4] MGM.

The Winged Monkeys are her second line of defense. The Monkeys are the big things that attack us. They are the deep dark secrets from our past that no one wants to look at. They are the things that tear apart our intellect and shut down our heart.

Dirty little secrets from our past give the monkeys their wings, and deep seated guilt and shame give them flight. These demons are born in the darkness of our subconscious and exist because of our unwillingness to look at them. We need only to fearlessly examine them to dispel their power.

Early on in my spiritual journey, I was actively involved in a twelve-step program. When it came time to do my fourth and fifth steps[5], I encountered the Winged Monkeys for the first time. This was a most intense experience for me because I had been harboring such guilt for the things I had done. I really thought that I was a bad person and the idea of going within and talking about these things was overwhelming.

As with most change in my life, it took a certain amount of pain before I was ready to move forward with these steps. I was terrified. I began to write out my fourth step and I remember my hands shaking because I was so nervous. I couldn't even think about what my fifth step would be like. I managed to get it all out. Every last secret I could think of.

I then went to my sponsor's house and prepared to share all my dirt with him. To my surprise, he stopped me and shared his fifth step with me. At first I thought he was not clear on the concept, but I later realized that he was putting my mind at ease. As I listened to him, I realized

---

[5] Steps 4 and 5 are:
    4. Made a searching and fearless moral inventory of ourselves.
    5. Admitted to God, to ourselves and to another human being the exact nature of our wrongs.

that there was nothing that he had done that changed who he was. His dirt contributed to his own willingness to forget his identity, but only for as along as he was willing to keep things locked away in the dark corners of his mind.

When he finished, I shared my list with him. It was such a relief. The Winged Monkeys of my mind became timid and shy. They no longer had the power to terrorize me and cripple me with fear. The light of awareness once again dispelled the shadows of my mind.

The Winkies are her third and final line of defense. The Winkies are the soldiers that guard her castle and chant that strange OEO chant. The Winkies represent the part of our psyche that exists in a pure state of fear and torment. The other levels of her defense, the Insects and the Monkeys, had discernable events and characteristics associated with them. The Winkies exist in a state of pure fear. They are imprisoned in the Witch's castle and never leave.

The fear they represent has to do with our basic fear of home. You see, the Winkies are much like the Munchkins who were enslaved by the Witch of the East. They were good folks who existed in a peaceful state until they were enslaved. They don't like their behavior, but they don't seem to have any choice. The mindless chanting is all they feel capable of.

This is what happens to most of us when we enter the Witch's castle. The part of us that feels trapped by her spell stands before us and fills our mind with a droning chant to the ego. There is no one thing with which to identify our fear, but it is very real. Perhaps it is because we are so close to transcendence that we want to recoil in fear.

There is nothing logical about this level of our ego defense. It is fear of the known and fear of the unknown. It is fear of God and the fear that maybe there is no God. It is fear of our vulnerability and fear of our power. To be surrounded by the Witch's henchmen is the most crippling feeling. It is, in the Witch's words, being trapped like mice.[6]

There is no easy way to describe this experience. I suspect it is the experience that a person has when they have a nervous breakdown, or that Jesus had just before his death on the cross.[7] There is no one thing that is pushing us to our knees—simply the realization that everything can be snatched from our grasp.

Interestingly, this can be a very powerful and decisive moment in our growth. By having everything taken from us, all means of psychological rationalization removed from the realm of possibility, we have the opportunity to surrender to the power of the Spirit, and in that surrender we have the opportunity to win our freedom.

In the end, it is the Winkies who give Dorothy the broom. In the end, they are her allies. These, the darkest demons in our mind, turn out to be our most valued allies in the long run. And it happens when we allow ourselves to come face to face with the Witch herself.

# Liquidation

*"Oh, you liquidated her, eh? Very resourceful."*

—The Wizard (MGM)

Transcending the ego is the goal of any spiritual path, though it may be described in very different ways. Whatever the process is called, it is always the same internal experience. It is the return to Oneness. It is an understanding that all beings emanate from one source and that this source

---

[6] MGM.
[7] Mark 15:34.

is where an individual's value and power originate.

Dorothy's experience of transcending the ego is symbolized in the melting of the Wicked Witch. In Oz terminology, liquidation and transcendence are synonymous. Throughout the story, the Witch terrorizes Dorothy. She threatens her and her friends and always makes a dramatic entrance and exit. Dorothy has to stand up to the Witch to dissolve her power.

In our lives we have the same challenge that faced Dorothy . The Wicked Witch who terrorizes our minds gets her power from our fear. It doesn't matter what form the fear takes. She grows in strength every time we step away from the edge of the unknown. Her nails grow longer and sharper every time we settle for the status quo. Her cackle gets louder and more nerve splitting every time we choose ignorance over wisdom.

There are two kinds of fear. One is a self-preservation mechanism put into our psyche by our Spirit. It tells us when to get out of a situation. It is the part of us that, in a sixth sense sort of way, knows when we are in danger. There are countless stories of people who have been mugged and say that in hindsight they knew something was wrong or that they wanted to get away from where they were. In most cases people ignore this feeling, believing it is all in their heads. Usually it is not.

The other kind of fear is of the ego. It is not a rational fear, but rather an illogical paranoia that keeps us stuck in our pain and suffering. It is this ego fear that prevents us from going home, or even making life in Oz all that it can be. As long as we submit to this fear, we will be slaves to the Wicked Witch. She knows this, and she will stop at nothing to make sure we don't examine her fear tactics too closely, because once we do, we will see that there is nothing there at all.

Our Spirit has the sole goal of getting us home with a minimal amount of suffering. Suffering is of the ego, and when we are experiencing pain or discomfort, you can be sure we are not following the counsel of Spirit. This is not to say that when we follow the Spirit we will not encounter difficult and painful situations. We most certainly will, for our Spirit leads us to them, so we can walk through the door and be through with it altogether.

Living in the Castro district[8] of San Francisco, I have seen many people deal with grief due to the AIDS epidemic. It is interesting to see how different people deal with this intense emotion. For some, there is a suffering that rips through their soul and batters them with fear. For others, death is a spiritual experience. It is a liberation, not just for the soul crossing over, but for all those who knew and loved him or her. In both cases the intense emotion of grief is present, but the experience of it is very different. When it is filtered though the ego, it is experienced as suffering, and when it is guided by Spirit, it is experienced as liberation.

The fear that the ego creates to keep us in bondage is also the gate that leads to the lawns of heaven.[10] At some point we need to walk through that fear. We need to go into the uncomfortable. We need to visit the awkward and the undesirable. The Witch is like an axe-wielding maniac, or so we believe. The axe that she uses to chase us is our fear of pain, our fear of the unknown, and our fear of adversity. When we walk headlong into these things, liberation comes and her axe becomes a bouquet of flowers.

It is this fear that radiates out into our lives and affects everything we do—from the addictions and obsessions which sabotage much of what we do, to outright fear of

[8] The Castro district is the hub of the gay community in the USA and is considered to be ground zero for the AIDS epidemic.
[10] *A Course in Miracles.*

some monster that has numerous arms—each arm representing things like the IRS, job security, health and relationships.

For most of us, it is fear rather than faith that guides our decisions. Many don't even see things as a choice. They think it is a given that you will be repelled by your spouse and eventually divorce, hate your job, and struggle to pay the bills. A one-week vacation each year is the only thing some people have to look forward to. Sadly, few question this way of life.

My father called me once on a Sunday morning. It was a beautiful day and I was on my way to the beach. We had a nice conversation about our lives and I shared with him how happy I was with my work and with life in general. Then he said, with a hint of sarcasm, something that I did not expect: "It must be nice to spend your life enjoying yourself."

My response was simply, "It is, I recommend it to everyone." My life is wonderful, but I truly believe that it is because I made some difficult decisions, and I continue to make them. While many of my friends were doing the responsible thing by choosing to pursue careers that would ensure a safe future with a nice nest egg for retirement, I chose to pursue the "follow my bliss"[11] path.

I decided early on that I would rather die regretting the things I had done than the things I had not done. This path of following the guidance of Spirit rather than the irrational fear of the ego is the bucket of water that liquidates the Witch. She has no power over us when we walk into these fears, because they are all smoke and mirrors. They do nothing but keep us in bondage. When we work for Spirit, our job security is guaranteed for eternity. Food and

---

[11] Joseph Campbell used this phrase many times.

shelter are always provided (though not always in the way we expect), and our relationships bring us far more smiles than tears.

When we really face the Witch and take a stand against her mind-freezing cackling, she and all the fear she inspired melt away, and we are free.

# Chapter Five

# The Scarecrow

## Getting off Your Post

*"Oh, I'm not feeling very well. You see, it's very tedious being stuck up here all day long with a pole up your back."*

—The Scarecrow (MGM)

The Scarecrow represents our intellect. He is our thinking self—the part of us that can figure and configure. He is the part of us that sees a blank canvas as a potential painting and then tells the body how to make it happen. He is our brain—the part of us that will travel with us through this life, helping us navigate our way through Oz. There is almost no situation where he cannot be of help.

Unfortunately his skills and talents can be used by the Wicked Witch as well as by the Good Witch, and that is why learning to use the mind in a constructive way is so essential to our spiritual growth and wellbeing. When the Scarecrow is enslaved by the Witch, varying degrees of hell are sure to follow.

Our first step in getting the Scarecrow to work with us rather than against us is to take him off his post. The Wicked Witch is very content to have him on that post. She knows that until he is taken down his ability to help Dorothy is nonexistent. As long as our brains are kept occupied with busywork such as scaring crows, they are virtually useless.

In the book, Scarecrow is placed on a post by a Munchkin farmer. His job is simply to sit there and scare crows away. As you may recall from Chapter One, the Munchkins represent our childhood tribe. And they are usually the origin of our brain being used as a post-it note. Everyone's childhood is different of course, but many of us were never encouraged to think for ourselves.

We were told to memorize our multiplication tables, and to remember that in 1492 Columbus sailed the ocean blue, but most were not encouraged to think for ourselves. Even in many art classes children are told what to create.

Thinking for yourself is against almost every social code we have. Boys can't wear pink and cook, and girls can't climb trees or play football. As a child I would ask adults about rules such as these and I would get the famous "Because I said so!" reply that makes no sense whatsoever.

What is most tragic about this is not the fact that for the rest of their lives little boys are afraid of the color pink , although it certainly has its repercussions. The real tragedy is that we are told not to think. Instead we are asked to put our common sense, logic and creativity on hold and never to question the way things are. This is the Wicked Witch's best defense against our individual and collective evolution.

There was a movie called *Wag the Dog* which got terrible reviews, perhaps because it was uncomfortably true to life. Like in the movie, we are told what we think we want to hear and we accept it as truth. We are told by our educational institutions what to think. The medical profession tells us what drugs to take. Religions tell us what to believe and how to behave, and politicians keep telling us to look at how misguided the people from other political parties are, so that their own selfish interests won't be exposed.

Learning to think for oneself is a dangerous game. Falling off that post when the soul turns the nail[1] can leave us with a few bruises. It is easy to rationalize that the view isn't half bad up there, and the job security can't be beat. But while these things may be true, the job satisfaction leaves a bit to be desired. The post is a safe place to be, but it is death any way you slice it. With the mind dead, the body and soul have little choice but to follow.

When we start to think for ourselves, some wonderful things happen. First, we become a player in the game instead of a pawn. We begin to have a say in how our reality unfolds. The more our brains begin to wake up, the more we begin to take responsibility for our lives, our communities and our world.

It is certainly easier to keep the mind nailed to the post. We can blame the President or the Congress or big business for all the evils in the world. Around kitchen tables and at cafés, gathered around the backs of pick-up trucks and sitting in bars, people are talking about politics, the environment and social issues. The question we should be asking ourselves is, "Why? Why are we still talking about these issues?" The issues haven't changed except perhaps to grow in magnitude. Action is needed and the seeds of free thought give rise to to healing.

I once saw a clear example of this when I went to see Hillary Clinton speak. During her speech, a group of

---

[1] In the movie, the scarecrow falls from his post when Dorothy turns the nail which holds him.

pro-life protesters came marching up behind me chanting and yelling. Aside from being rude, they looked like drones. They might just as well have been a pro-choice group, because of the obvious mindlessness with which this protest was carried out. It didn't seem to matter what side they were chanting for. It was clear that this was not a protest about abortion, but rather a stirring up of emotions based on a very divisive issue.

After the speech, I spoke with one of the protesters who made no bones about her dislike for the Clintons. She felt that they were responsible for the deaths of thousands of innocent lives. Now, I could have respected her opinion if I had felt it was her own, but I felt it was simply rehashed pro-life propaganda. Because I didn't think her opinions were her own, I asked her some very basic questions to test my theory.

"How many children have you adopted?"

"Well, none."

"How many pregnant teenage girls have you brought into your home to give them the support they need to bring a pregnancy to term?"

"None."

"Well surely you must visit the hospital and hold the tiny crack babies that benefit so much from loving human touch."

"No, I don't. Do you do all these things?"

"No, but I am not the one interrupting Mrs. Clinton, who has dedicated much of her public influence to helping children."

She went away in a huff. My goal was not to promote the Clintons or to argue for the pro-choice movement.

I think much of the pro-choice movement is flawed as well. The point I was trying to make was that nothing will be solved by yelling and screaming words which someone else has put in our mouths. Sitting and really considering the problem at hand, and then taking action to solve it—that has the potential to heal.

A second benefit of getting off the post comes in the form of choice. In the Western world we have tremendous political freedom. We can choose between Lucky Charms and Wheaties, between Levis and Gap, between Catholic and Protestant or Judaism and Atheism, all within the context of safety. No one is going to throw us in prison for standing up and disagreeing with the President. No one is going to force us to worship in a specific church. We have, at least externally, all the freedom we could ask for.

This presents us with a real problem, however. One would think that with all this freedom, we would be happy—that there would be nothing to stop us from pursuits that would make our hearts sing with joy. But the sad reality is that people in the West are not happy, and it is rare that our hearts sing. Having everything we want and still being unhappy really is depressing, because it is not far from the painful admission that happiness is a personal decision. The pursuit of happiness[2] can be guaranteed by a document, but knowing where to search can only be guided by an open and freethinking mind.

Few of us can escape the lies that we are told about happiness. For each subculture the lie is a bit different, but as long as we believe the lie, we will be slaves. All the political freedom in the world is not going to change that. I think that an example is the best way to explain.

As we grow up we are told that happiness is found

---

[2] The Declaration of Independence.

through certain things. First, being popular in school. Then we are told that we will be happy when we finish college. Then we are told that we will find happiness when we marry. Of course the next step toward happiness is to have a child or children. Then we have retirement to look forward to. A nice neat package. A simple recipe that is sure to make us happy.

Not so. Some people will be popular in school and some will be unpopular; neither case guarantees happiness. Some people will go to college and others will not; neither course will come through on the promise of happiness. Some people's relationships will follow the traditional route and become a life-long commitment in marriage. Others will divorce or not marry at all. Happiness has nothing to do with these things, either. Children are a great joy and the choice to have them is a big one. But doing so to fill a void will not bring happiness either to the parents or the child. And retirement, the last holdout, is more often a time of bitterness than a time of joy.

Why is this? All of these events could be happy and full of joy. There is nothing wrong with choosing this path. But it will not bring happiness unless happiness is chosen above all else. Attachment to form must be let go. Here is where getting off the post comes in handy. When we think for ourselves, we can begin to decide what will make us happy. That may be a traditional path or it may be off the wall, but it will be a free choice based on the deep longing of the heart (more about that in the next chapter). The key is to have the open-mindedness to follow your bliss.[3]

Perhaps a person will choose travel over attending college or choose to be in an open relationship instead of marriage. The choice is what is at stake here. Getting off

[3] Joseph Campbell.

the post is what gives us that choice, and the freedom that comes with it. No prison can squelch that kind of freedom and no political structure can guarantee it. It is a freedom that exists deep inside, and while we can be encouraged to forget this gift, it can never be taken from us.

## Some People Do an Awful Lot of Talking

*"I don't know, but some people without brains do an awful lot of talking—don't they?"*

—*The Scarecrow (MGM)*

The development of the intellect is a noble pursuit to be sure, but it is only the first step in using the brain for the advancement of the soul. There have been men and women throughout history who have had superior intellect, but were lacking in common sense and wisdom. They had the know-how to accomplish many great things, but they failed to see the simplicity of universal spiritual laws.

The raising of awareness is our next step in the development of our intellect. The learning phase we experience when we get off our posts can be likened to the laying of an egg. The potential for life is there, but that potential may end in an omelet if the next phase, raising awareness, is not cultivated. The raising of awareness can be likened to the incubation period in which the mind begins to mature and cultivate the freethinking that was gained earlier.

To raise awareness is not easy. It means being conscious and present to everything—from the small stuff like breathing to the big stuff like the environmental breakdown that threatens our planet. It means looking squarely at many of the uncomfortable things that would be easier to sweep under the rug. It means embracing the whole of life rather than denying the parts that are awkward and uncomfortable.

Living a conscious and aware life means walking head first into the present moment and viewing, without judgment, whatever it is that lies before you. This consciousness is not easy because it demands we own our experience and not push the responsibility off onto someone else. It asks us to acknowledge our mistakes, but it also gives us the opportunity to learn from them so that we can grow and evolve, turning our mistakes into lessons.

There are three main areas where we need to raise awareness: emotional, mental and physical. These levels need to begin with the individual and then quickly move outward to the rest of the world. On all of these levels, we have the opportunity to grow and heal ourselves, our society and our planet.

Raising awareness about emotions is the hardest for some people, because emotions are not easy to grab onto. There is nothing tangible to wrap our mental fingers around. Add to that the fact that there is nothing logical about emotions. Just trying to identify them is hard. Rarely do we experience pure emotions. They are most often like a multi-layer marble cake. Swirls of anger mix easily with jealousy. Happiness seems to mix well with love. Fear and love, our two root emotions, often dance together as well. And through all this confusion, our Spirit is asking us to be fully aware of what we are feeling.

One of my counseling clients, whom I will call Fran, was a compulsive over-eater. She spent much of her time hopping from support group to support group. In spite of her best efforts, she was unable to get her eating habits or weight under control for any length of time. So I asked her why she went to support groups.

"Because I have trouble getting in touch with my emotions," she replied.

"And has it helped?"

"Some, but I still have a lot of trouble with it."

I casually changed the subject for a while and then asked her if she would be willing to eat a conscious yogic diet. I then proceeded to tell her what that would entail. Immediately I could see her body shift nervously; she became apprehensive, and it was obvious that fear was the predominant emotion that was washing through her.

"So what are you feeling right now?" I asked.

"Total fear!"

"So does this count as getting in touch with your feelings?"

Fran is not unique in this way. Americans spend thousands of dollars on therapy and support groups. There are more twelve-step groups than college basketball teams, and mood-altering drugs such as Prozac are prescribed more often than aspirin. We say we want to get in touch with our emotions, but we have all these judgments about which ones are worthy of our awareness.

Right now, it is cool to get in touch with anger at parents, but contentment is brushed off as denial. Raising our awareness around emotions is both simple and dreadfully difficult. It is simple in that all you have to do is stop and notice what you are feeling. It doesn't have to be some grand and overwhelming emotion, though it may be. As you notice what you are feeling in this moment, simply feel it. Try not to figure it out. Remember, emotions are anything but logical. Simply identify what you are feeling and allow yourself to feel it as fully as possible. If you need to laugh or smile, go for it. If you need to cry, allow yourself to do that. There is no need to force a smile or tears. They will come when they need to. Simply become aware of what you are feeling and let it find its full expression.

The difficult part of this exercise is that we like to put things in nice neat boxes. We like to know why, and it is tempting to feel like there is something wrong with us if we are not feeling the right emotion. One of my mother's friends went to Atlantic City to gamble, only days after her husband's death. Some of her friends thought it was tacky and were berating her for doing it. Atlantic City is the last place I would want to go while in grief, but there is no wrong way to express emotions and everyone has his or her own way. The important thing is not in the how, so long as it is not harmful to ourselves or others. The only thing that matters from a spiritual point of view is that we do it with awareness.

Does this mean that counselors and support groups are bad? Of course not. But we are having emotions all day long. Getting in touch with them is as easy as sitting and feeling. Staying present to them is where outside support can be helpful. But that outside support should never try to define or dictate a person's feelings.

Raising awareness on a psychological level is not easy either. It means taking responsibility for our thoughts. Many of us go through life thinking all sorts of thoughts and believing we have no control over them. They just enter our consciousness with no seeming influence from us. When we see someone we don't like, we blame him or her for making us think such hateful thoughts. The reality is that we don't like them because of our thoughts and beliefs about them.

While visiting a yoga ashram, I met this beautiful

woman. We had an amazing connection and I fell in love. Even now I smile thinking about her. It was quite a special time. She too, had strong feelings for me, but when it came time to deepen the relationship by moving closer together, she decided it was not what she wanted. I was devastated.

In addition to the emotions I was feeling, I had wild judgments and fantasies swirling through my head. Should I jump in the car and go see her? Should I never speak to her again? I wanted to call her a bitch and I wanted to call her a goddess. I was going crazy. I felt like I had no control over my own mind.

I tried to meditate, but focusing was seemingly impossible, so I prayed. I asked only to see the truth about her. Instantly my mind shut up. I began to feel peace and compassion and my thoughts and beliefs about her shifted from frantic judgments to quiet thoughts of respect and honor.

It was months before I really understood what happened that afternoon. I had made a choice to own my thoughts rather than letting my ego mind go wild. She was no longer taking up space in my head rent-free.[4]

Owning our thoughts is not easy. Our thoughts are like knee-jerk[5] reactions. Most of us tend to think reflexively rather than progressively. Taking responsibility for our thoughts is not impossible, however, and elevating our awareness about what we are thinking is where we begin this process. Once we do this, choice is again ours, and beating the Victim Drum is no longer necessary.

The body, in theory, should be the easiest place to raise awareness because it is so gross and tangible. Being a yoga instructor, I have seen that it is a very difficult place

---

[4] Based on a saying popular in Alcoholics Anonymous.
[5] A concept discussed by Dan Millman in his book, *Way of the Peaceful Warrior.*

for people to maintain awareness. In fact, body awareness is the area that I focus on most with my beginner students.

Our bodies know exactly what they need. If you listen to your body, it will tell you when it is hungry, tired or ill. It will also tell you exactly what it requires to remedy the situation. Given the right nutrients, rest and exercise, I believe the body has the ability to remedy almost any situation. In order to give it what it needs, however, we need to be aware of it long enough to hear what it is asking for.

Most people find themselves in my yoga class because they are in pain. To a greater or lesser degree, their bodies appear to be the enemy causing them pain and discomfort. Once they start to practice and the awareness of the body deepens, they start to realize that the body was not the enemy; it was just screaming for relief. Living the American lifestyle is not conducive to much other than developing heart disease, cancer and chronic pain. Once people get back into their bodies they start to hear the wisdom.

Diets get cleaned up, jobs get modified to reduce stress, lives get simplified and the breath gets deeper. People, friends and co-workers, start to notice a softer smile and eyes that are more bright and full of some mysterious light. In short, healing occurs, and it is all based on a heightened awareness of the body.

We can take all the pills in the world or take herbs and vitamins, or become acupuncture pincushions, and none of these will do a thing unless they are accompanied with a greater awareness of the body. To be sure, with awareness these things can help the body to heal, but not without it.

When we meditate or participate in any spiritual practice, we raise awareness. That is the primary goal. Until we are aware of the problem, there is no chance we will be able to change. We will be doomed to repeat the past. With awareness we have a choice. We may choose to be angry or to hold negative thoughts or to eat French fries, but it will be a choice. In time we learn the rewards and consequences of such choices and we will start to make more wise decisions.

## The Doctor of Thinkology

*"Why, anybody can have a brain. That's a very mediocre commodity. Every pusillanimous creature that crawls on the earth or slinks through the slimy seas has a brain. Back where I come from, we have universities, seats of great learning, where men go to become great thinkers. And when they come out, they think great thoughts, and with no more brains than you have. But they have got one thing you haven't got, a diploma."*

—*The Wizard (MGM)*

There is a great demand in our culture to educate ourselves. We place a great deal of emphasis on a college education. Without a diploma, the chances of success within the framework of the established workforce are greatly lessened. It would appear that a college diploma is as essential to success today as a high school diploma was forty years ago.

I am a strong advocate of education in the formal sense. I truly believe that K through twelve schools in the United States are a disgrace and that our number one priority should be the education of the younger generation. But I also feel that it is important not to overrate a piece of paper. A diploma may represent years of hard work, but it is no replacement for wisdom.

When the Wizard gives the Scarecrow his diploma, the Scarecrow says, "The sum of the square roots of any two sides of an isosceles triangle is equal to the square root of the remaining side." As a child, I never knew what he was talking about. Even after I learned a thing or two about geometry, I didn't give it much thought. Then, while doing research for this book, I came across a great web site[6] filled with great Oz facts. On it I learned that the real equation, which was assumed to be the Pythagorean Theorem, was "The sum of the squares of the legs of a right triangle is equal to the square of the hypotenuse."

The exact equation is not important, and whether or not MGM did this on purpose I have no idea, but it is highly symbolic of a great misconception between wisdom and intellect. There are a large number of people who can figure out complex equations or program computers, but can't function in day-to-day life. There are people who can't balance a checkbook, but have a wisdom that is obvious to even a casual observer.

The issue of the diploma is one of validation. When we jump through certain hurdles and prove we have acquired a certain amount of knowledge, we are given a piece of paper that states such. This paper in and of itself means nothing. It merely represents the knowledge we acquired.

The Scarecrow's diploma was not about raw intellect. If it were, he would have known the geometry equation. Rather it represents his wisdom. In and of itself it holds no power. But it does symbolize all the lessons he learned as he walked through Oz.

Wisdom is a blend of logic and intuition. It is the result

6 This website is hosted by Eric Gjovaag and can be found at http://www.eskiom.com/~tiktok/

of learning lessons in the school of life. It is the means by which we avoid pitfalls and learn new lessons with greater ease. It is the understanding that lets us appreciate life with all its weird quirks and intricacies, and in that gratitude dance our way though life in a perfect balance of give and take.

Wisdom needs no piece of paper to back it up. It carries with it a contentment that requires no external documentation. Yet having it validated in some way seems to strengthen and tone it. The Scarecrow's diploma represents this validation.

This diploma comes in many forms. It is the joy of knowing what truth to speak to heal a conflict. It is the surrender that is felt when ending a relationship consciously. It is the serenity that comes when we learn to turn life's little traffic jams over to God. It is the satisfaction that comes with knowing when to speak and when to be silent.

This diploma is not the same as getting a college diploma, for it is a 100% internal experience. It serves as both a reward and a reminder for the value and efforts of living a conscious life with an open mind and willing heart. We may not be able to hang wisdom's diploma on an office wall, but the walls of our lives get decorated with its colorful rewards, and few can miss its distinctive mark.

Cultivating wisdom involves developing two very distinct intellectual skills—logic and intuition. Logic is something that few people really appreciate and it often gets confused with its nemesis. . . fear. Logic would never let us live unsatisfying lives filled with boredom and pain. Logic would have us recognize the brevity of our lives and allow us to make the most of them. Logic would never tell us to destroy our lives with drugs, unhealthy food, high stress jobs and life-draining relationships.

Cultivating logic allows us to get off our butts and take control of our lives. It recognizes that all the answers are right there in front of us. It honors emotion, but is not guided solely by its changing tides and shifting currents. Instead it raises the sails and lets the winds of life guide us through every situation.

Using logic means spreading the pieces of our life before us and putting them together with order and reason like a giant jigsaw puzzle. First, our logic has us find the edges and then gradually fills in the center until the mosaic of our life forms a radiant whole.

Logic is never closed-minded. In fact it is the most open-minded state we can assume. It always looks for new ways to solve old problems, while always drawing on past experiences to avoid recurring pitfalls. Logic will not allow for fundamentalism in any form, be it religious, scientific or secular. It is clean and straightforward and always ready to re-explore its past decisions and evaluations.

Intuition, the other hand that works for the mind, listens to the subtle guidance of Spirit. It trusts in what it hears in the quiet moments of contemplation and reflection. It comes in the form of a gut feeling or a quiet knowing. It manifests in dreams and visions. It is rarely as tangible as its sister logic, but is every bit as useful.

Cultivating intuition is as simple as shutting up. The universe is flowing through us like water through the gills of a fish. It is in us and around us. It sustains us and carries us. The immense wisdom of the universe is within us always, and intuition is the way we tap into it to hear its gentle whisper.

Intuition and logic seem to oppose each other at times, but that is only because one or the other is temporarily less developed. At their highest expression they are the same, for they come from the same mind. They are the alpha and the omega. Logic shows us the writing on the wall and intuition lets us listen to the voice of the one who wrote it.

As we nurture and develop these gifts, we become wise. The world bends around us and arranges itself to honor our efforts, and the result is a spiritual diploma that reminds us, and all who encounter us, that there is a better way to live—that there is a way home, and that an open mind will help us find it.

# Chapter 6

# The Tin Man

*"It's empty. The tinsmith forgot to give me a heart."*

—Tin Man (MGM)

The Tin Man represents the heart—the home of love and in love's absence, fear. Love is the essence of who we are. As much as this sounds like a cliché, it is so very true. Love is our ultimate reality and when we are not experiencing love or one of its many branches such as joy, happiness, contentment and serenity, we have forgotten the essence of who we are and where our value lies.

Fear is the baseline emotion from which all other negative emotions spring. Hatred, apathy, anger and jealousy are all expressions of fear. Fear comes solely from the belief that our love is limited or lacking in some way. The journey of the Tin Man then, is to discover that he is indeed capable of feeling love, and that love is not something that shines on him from without, but rather radiates from deep within him.

# Oiling a Rusty Heart

*"Look, he's rusted again. Get me the oil can quick!"*

—Dorothy (MGM)

The human heart is the most illogical thing in the human experience. It is the part of each human that offers us the greatest joy and the deepest sadness. Some would argue that the higher brain sets us apart from the animals, but I believe it is the heart. Animals have no separation between cognition and feeling. Humans, on the other hand, try to judge and analyse emotions—a very futile pursuit.

The heart allows us to feel emotions in such a rich and full way. It is the home of compassion and charity, love and tenderness. It is the place where we feel loss and the place where we feel so full of joy that it trickles over the top like a waterfall in a Zen garden. It is a sacred space that is filled with all the mystery and wonder of an entire universe, and it exists within each of us.

The Tin Man represents the heart. Like many of us, he has been tricked into believing that he has no heart—that his capacity to love is somehow hindered or non-existent. The world tells us over and over again that success in this world is about taking care of ourselves. It is about being competitive. It is about doing whatever it takes to survive, and to do this we must shut down our hearts. The shutting down of our hearts is what causes rust and corruption.

Our culture has pierced the hearts of many with a double-edged sword. One edge of this sword is the lie that love is a limited resource—that if I love you, I will not have enough love left for someone else. This lie, perhaps the biggest lie, has done untold damage. While the damage is horrendous, it is not irreversible.

I am the oldest of three children. When my mother was pregnant with my brother Jason, I remember feeling threatened by his imminent arrival in my family. Up until that time I was the center of my parent's universe. All of their love seemed to be pointed at me. Knowing he was going to get some of that love was not a comforting thought to my young mind.

When he was born, I discovered something interesting. My mother and father still loved me as much as ever. They still loved me unconditionally. But they also loved him with the same intensity. Their capacity to love had grown. The lesson I learned was that in love there is no lack.

Love is not of this world. It cannot be found in a box of chocolates or in great sex. It is otherworldly. Evidence of its existence can be found everywhere, but it doesn't play by the rules of the physical universe.

For example, if you have a gallon of water and you give a cup to a friend, you will no longer have a full gallon of water. If you were to keep doing that, your container would soon be empty.

Love, on the other hand, is very different. It cannot be measured by any scale we have because it is so different. When we give away some of our love, we are filled up again. When that love is received, the love is expanded and increased. If it is not received, it lies dormant like a bulb in the frozen earth waiting to bloom. No one lost, and everyone gained.

The rusted heart happens when we try to fit love into a neat little box, or when we try to define it in terms that should only be used in a physical context. In short order, we learn that love doesn't play by the rules we set forth, and when we try to force it, we get burned. Rather than open the mind to new possibilities, we shut the heart down and allow it to rust and decay.

The other edge of the sword is the promise that special love[1] is enough to bring us fulfillment. Romantic love in the harlequin sense is a big lie created by our egos. The lie is an offshoot of the first lie—that love is limited. Our soul needs love in order to survive. If all love were withdrawn from it by the ego, we would wake up.

Love is to the soul what oxygen is to the body. Without love the soul would die. Luckily, the soul is as eternal as its creator, so death is impossible. Withdrawing all love from the soul is like trying to suffocate yourself by holding your breath. You would turn purple and pass out, and then you would start breathing again automatically.

The soul is much the same way. If the Wicked Witch were to withdraw love altogether, we would wake up and she would be out of a job. So to remedy this, she gives us limited amounts of love. Just enough to keep us spiritually alive, but never enough to bring us the real love of which we are capable.

For most of us, this comes in the form of romantic love, or at least the hope for romantic love. The ego convinces us that to be complete, we need to find that special someone, and when we do we will feel contentment at last. In doing this, she infuses just enough hope into our existence to keep us from looking for something greater.

This romantic mumbo jumbo is not really love at all. It's more like a synthetic sweetener. It is artificial, leaves a bad aftertaste, and most likely causes disease.

This may be taken in a depressing light. For those who believe in true love, you may want to snap this book shut,

---

[1] A concept that is largely focused on in *A Course in Miracles*.

or wonder what awful thing happened in my life to give me this bitter edge. After all, if there were no true love, what would be the point of life?

I do believe in true love, and I believe it can be expressed in a romantic way. In fact, for a great many people, that is where it will be most clearly felt. But the approach to true love is different when it is motivated by the Spirit, rather than the ego.

The Spirit would have us experience romantic love as a platform from which we could experience true love with all beings. From the Spirit's point of view, falling in love with one person is just the tip of the iceberg. For as wonderful as it feels to look into your beloved's eyes, imagine how powerful the feeling would be to experience that in all eyes.

It is not that our Spirit wants us to love our partner less. Spirit would never ask us to love anyone less. Spirit always encourages us to love more. There is an ongoing call in our hearts to open up, be filled with the divine and let us share the grace of God with all beings. Our romantic relationships are just one form of that love.

It is not just in romance that this fencing off happens. It happens with our children, with our parents, with friends and family. Collectively it happens with religious, national and ethnic groups.

I once heard Pat Buchanan say that he felt the United States' policy on China was too lax because of their human rights violations. Normally, I disagree with his politics, so I was surprised to find myself agreeing with him. Then he said to the reporter, "I mean, they are killing Christians over there."

I understand his concern for human rights. It is my chief concern when it comes to casting my vote each

November, but to limit my concern to one group of people is to place a limit on my capacity to love. It is certainly a start, but just a beginning at that.

The human heart's capacity to love is only limited by a person's unwillingness to forgive. To limit the human heart in any way denies a person the greatest joy possible, and denies the world the greatest gift that can be offered.

As we start to pull this double-edged sword from our hearts, we begin to bleed, and that blood washes away the rust from our hearts. It oils us and gets our hearts back in working order.

# Bang on My Chest

*"Bang on my chest if you think I'm perfect.*
*Go ahead, bang on it!"*

—Tin Man (MGM)

Like the Tin Man, most people feel empty inside. This is not really big news to anyone who has done any amount of soul searching. Most people who are reasonably conscious can see that there is a nagging emptiness in most human hearts.

This emptiness is the cornerstone of the Wicked Witch's castle. It is the hollow ache that chases us through life, never really allowing us to experience our highest potential. It is the part of our being that yearns to be filled.

As I have already mentioned, this void can be filled only with love. Anything else will not nourish our hearts or souls. The sex, food and drugs can only serve to deny our pain, not alleviate it.

Paradoxically, it is this emptiness that is the key to our being filled. When the Tin Man asks Dorothy to bang on his chest, he opens himself up and becomes vulnerable. He shows the world that he feels empty and less than. It is only after he does this that he is able to begin the process of filling his emptiness.

The Tin Man's vulnerability is his strength, and therein lies the paradox. This is the same as saying, "The meek shall inherit the earth"[2] or stating, "'I, of myself, can do nothing,' is to gain all the power in the Universe."[3]

The power of letting the heart be open and raw is the process of running wild, naked and free. When we show our fear, our loneliness and our insecurity, we free ourselves from them. We retire from the full time job of hiding our emptiness from ourselves and the world and we begin to feel our hearts filling.

Most people operate under the belief, whether consciously or unconsciously, that to let the world see their vulnerability is to invite personal destruction and be crushed. So we spend a fortune on cosmetic surgery, makeup and clothes, sport utility vehicles and beer in a feeble attempt to hide this emptiness.

We put up facades for everyone to see. We are like a Hollywood set—perfectly manicured, but lacking in any depth. We rush from store to store, from trend to trend and from distraction to distraction, hoping that no one will see how empty we really feel. Of course few people ever buy the charade and only the really numb believe it about themselves.

When we stop all this nonsense, we hear a terrifying echo in the chamber of the heart. It ripples out like a pebble

---

[2] Matthew 5:5.
[3] A Course In Miracles.

tossed into the center of a pond, but out of that echo arises a love and a peace that cannot be taken away. By exposing our vulnerability, we are inoculated from it. The power that people and institutions once had over us is nullified, because we no longer seek validation from an outside source. We are filled from within.

To be vulnerable is to gain power and freedom. Not the power and freedom that armies and political institutions can offer, but rather a power that is otherworldly and without price.

The film *Schindler's List* provides a great example of this principle. In the movie, about half way through, there are three scenes that are shown together. The first shows Schindler, a wealthy, womanizing businessman with beautiful women hanging all over him. He is drinking and having a great time.

At the same time, the general in charge of the prison camp is shown with his Jewish maid. It is obvious that he loves her, but has shut down his heart so much that he feels fear and anger. He blames her for his vulnerability.

A third scene shows a young Jewish couple getting married in the prison camp. They have nothing. But they are obviously deeply in love.

These three scenes show something really powerful. Neither the General nor Schindler have really felt the tenderness of the human heart. Both have a great deal of power. The General decides when people live and when people die and wields his power without any sense of right and wrong. Schindler has all the money he could hope for. Physical pleasure and material comfort are his companions. But neither of these men has what the two enslaved teens have.

They are the most vulnerable and the most raw.

On an earthly level, every comfort and dignity has been taken from them, but the fullness and richness of their hearts can not be taken from them. No prison can contain it; not even death can interrupt it.

To be open and vulnerable is to spread the wings of freedom. The knowledge and wisdom of the Scarecrow pointed to the direction and application of the powerful shoes. The vulnerability and tenderness of the Tin Man allows for a space where the Good Witch can fill the soul and lead Dorothy gently along her path.

## The Breaking Heart

*"Now I know I have a heart because it's breaking."*

—The Tin Man (MGM)

Grief is one of the most dreaded human emotions. We do everything we can to avoid facing death. Yet we die each moment only to be reborn in the next. Change is the nature of Spirit's self expression. Its shifting forms are not Spirit itself, but rather Spirit seeking to express itself in new ways. Spirit doesn't exist in time and space any more than an artist exists within his or her canvas. But Spirit's gentle mark is left on the canvas of the physical universe with each brush stroke.

My best friend Michael always says, "No man can get into the same river twice." This is the essence of the Tin Man's grief. This is the cause of his breaking heart. It is the attachment to form that causes our pain and reminds us of our true capacity to love. Were it not for grief we would be content to believe we were a shallow pond rather than a great ocean.

Grief is often thought of as a negative emotion because of the intense pain associated with it. This is a confusion that is understandable but unfortunate. Negative emotions always involve a shutting down of the heart—be they anger, rage, jealousy or whatever. When we feel these emotions our hearts are in the process of closing. This is not to say there is something wrong with feeling negative emotions, but not working through them in a timely manner makes for layers of rust.

Grief is a heart opening. It is a surrender of the way we thought things were and an opening up to the greater truth behind them. It is a lifting up of our hearts. When we experience grief, our heart is growing in its capacity to love, and with that growth come growing pains. Much like the Grinch whose heart grew three sizes on Christmas morning, our hearts expand when we experience loss.

The growth of our heart happens as we say goodbye to impermanence and say hello to the eternal nature that exists within all beings. Human love is wonderful, but it is limited because it is conditional. It is based on shared experiences, physical forms, and ideas about what things should look like. When we experience a loss in one of these human forms, not only is the love we shared still present, but it often grows because it is no longer limited by a set form.

When I was in college, I visited the Museum of Art at the Rhode Island School of Design, where several Tibetan Monks had come to build one of their famous Sand Mandalas. It took them hours and hours of concentration and work. Little by little they would sprinkle colored sand in perfect amounts. Over the course of months, these monks created a very large and beautiful work of art. As part of their spiritual practice, they then took the finished Mandala down to the Providence River and dumped it in. The whole process was something to see. To work so hard on something and then let it go was a real lesson for me to witness.

"Jesus wept."[4] is the shortest sentence in the whole Bible, yet it speaks volumes about what it means to be spiritually evolved. Jesus, by anyone's standards, had his act together. Whether he is viewed as a historical or a mythical figure—whether a person looks at him as the Son of God or as a man, he represents, here in the West anyway, the potential that all humans have.

At the height of human potential, Jesus wept. There are no apologies for this weeping, and no rationalization for it. It is a simple and clear statement. Jesus' friend Lazarus had died and he was grieving—allowing his heart to be open to loving Lazarus in a new way.

Grief is a powerful emotion and when we allow ourselves to experience it fully, we grow and expand as individuals. It is the fire that burns away the chaff[5] in our minds. It is the ultimate in surrender and its sweet reward is serenity.

---

[4] John 11:35.
[5] Matthew 3:12.

## Chapter Seven

# The Lion

If anyone ever tells you that the spiritual life is easy, they have not walked the yellow brick road for long. The journey from Munchkin Village to our gentle awakening in Kansas is not easy, and the seeming uncertainty of it all can be very fearful. There is nothing that can change the fearful nature of this journey; it is a fact that should not be avoided or sugar coated. But courage can help us to look through the illusions that rattle the cages of our mind.

It takes tremendous courage to walk the spiritual path with integrity and honor. No one relishes the thought of leaving the familiar surroundings of our Munchkin childhood. No one looks forward to a journey into the Witch's castle. These things scare us to death, but courage allows us to rise out of that fear, into life. It takes courage to step up to the plate and walk head first into our deepest fears.

# Kings and Slaves

*"What makes a King out of a Slave?"*

*Lion (MGM)*

In one of his songs, the Lion asks, "What makes a King out of a Slave?" and answers, "Courage!"[1] And he was quite right. Courage is the key that unlocks the shackles around our feet—shackles put there by the Wicked Witch. These shackles are what prevent us from experiencing the richness of life. And the way to turn the key is to feel the fear and do it anyway.[2]

There are two kinds of fear, and learning to distinguish between the two is an essential part of developing courage. The first kind of fear tells us something is wrong, for instance, the fear of putting one's hand on a hot stove. This is a natural and legitimate fear, and it should be honored.

The other kind of fear is the irrational kind. It is the fear that keeps a woman with her abusive husband, and the fear that drives a person to drink. It is the fear that the devil we don't know is so much worse than the one we know all too well.

It is the fear of the known and the fear of the unknown. It is the fear of deceit and the even bigger fear of the truth. It is the fear of our weakness but even more it is the fear of our power.

It is this fear that keeps us from taking the bold steps along our yellow brick road that are necessary to return home. It is neither logical nor practical. It is nothing more than the rantings of an ego desperate to keep us in Oz and

[1] MGM
[2] *Feel the Fear and Do It Anyway* is a book by Susan Jeffers

usurp the power of our magic shoes.

There is only one way out of this fear and that is to go through it. Fear is the door that we must walk through. It is the gate of heaven, and it is only our lack of courage and faith that keeps us in bondage. Developing these things is our freedom and our salvation.

We have a choice in life. We can let the Wicked Witch sit at the center of our minds, ruling with her fearful cackle, or we can cultivate the courage it takes to oust her from power. As long as we allow her to sit there, she is the master and we are the slaves. When we look her square in the eye, we bump her to the side and take our rightful place as king. We become masters of our own lives, making choices that are inspired by Spirit and ushering in an era of freedom.

Courage and faith are two sides of the same coin. Faith creates a space for courage, and courage allows us to move forward, testing that faith and in turn strengthening it. Courage and faith are the two feet that allow us to walk through our fear to the freedom that lies just beyond it. There is a Hindu proverb that states: "Fear knocked at the door. Faith answered. No one was there."

This sums up what we must do every time we step to the edge of our fear. If we are to become kings rather than slaves, we must walk with courage. We must have faith that when we open fear's door and walk through, there will not be a tiger waiting to devour us, but rather a new freedom that would let us breathe easier and sleep more deeply.

My mother and father are two of the most beautiful human beings I have ever met, but I wouldn't wish their marriage on anyone. For twenty-five years they stayed together for the kids, or at least that is what they tried to make my brother, sister and me believe. In reality, they stayed together because of fear. My father was afraid of being alone, and my mother was afraid she couldn't support herself. When they finally separated, they both walked through their fears and came out the other side stronger and happier people. They were no longer trapped in a marriage that neither satisfied them nor gave them any real sense of protection. My father was alone long before the divorce, and my mother always struggled to pay the bills.

By walking through the fear, they were able to find new spouses who are much better suited for them. They both have found a greater degree of happiness and freedom which could never have been found by staying in the false security of a bad marriage.

The Lion was afraid and he confused that with a lack of courage. This was one of his lessons. Like the Lion, we will be frightened and we will feel fear. This will not change. But once we start to take bold steps into this fear, we will no longer be slaves to it.

## All for Dorothy

*"I'll go in there for Dorothy."*

—Lion (MGM)

In order to be truly courageous, we need a cause. Something to feel truly passionate about. Without this passionate commitment, it is unlikely that the commitment to walking through fear will be enough to carry us through.

There are many things to be committed to, of course— loyalty to family, state and church are just a few. For these causes one may be asked to fight and even die to preserve principle and property. The soul, when we get right down to it, asks for the same type of commitment.

Much like the soldier who is called to war, the Lion needed to face three main things in order to walk into the Witch's castle and free his friend. When the Lion decided to go into the Witch's castle for Dorothy, he was full of fear. His fear was justified in a sense, because win or lose, he was in for a difficult ride. If he failed, he would lose Dorothy. If he succeeded, Dorothy would be returning to Kansas.

When our souls call out for help, we need to face the what-ifs that distract us from the purpose of our life here on earth. We don't know what the future holds. We can never predict it of course, but somehow living a neurotic yet convenient existence gives us a certain amount of predictability. We can count on certain things, and even if those things are painful, they are familiar.

When the Lion in our minds decides to go into the dark places, change is sure to follow, and with any change comes a certain amount of unknown. I have heard stories about African Americans being opposed to the civil rights movement in the early sixties, which on the surface seems like a strange thing. But with civil rights came new ground. Generations of African Americans had been oppressed. Civil rights, while desirable, required a complete redefining of self. Black Americans were about to have a new role in society, and accepting that role must have taken tremendous courage.

Even Martin Luther King was a bit confused as to what the future would hold for Black America. On the night he was shot he said, "I don't know what will happen now. We've got some difficult days ahead." He, like every other African American, could barely imagine what their lives would be like with equal freedom and equal protection under the law. What made Martin Luther King, Jr. such a courageous leader, was not that he knew the future, but that he had his finger on the pulse of America's soul. He didn't know where things were going, but he did know that the soul of America was twisting in pain and needed to swallow a difficult pill if it were to find healing. It was his faith in Spirit that gave him this courage. He went on to say, "But it really doesn't matter to me now. Because I've been to the mountain top. . . And I've looked over, and I've seen the Promised Land."[3]

A similar fear that the Lion needed to walk through was his fear of death. For most, it is their pain and suffering that defines who they are. When we confront this, death occurs—not an easy thing to embrace. If I were to let go of my identity as a white, bisexual, American male yoga instructor with long hair, who would I be? How about all the pain in my life, the bitterness toward my parents or institutions or society? What would happen if I stopped identifying myself with all the things I have been told I was? What would be left?

When we let go of these things, we die. Or at least the part of us that is not eternal will die and in this death is freedom! "It is in dying that we are born to eternal life."[4] This is such an amazing truth—so very liberating—such a treasure. But in order to do this we need to have the courage to accept it.

In the instant that we let go of an identity based on finite things, our Spirit rushes to lift us up and show us that our identity and our value is so far beyond the limits we set on ourselves. Glinda (or Spirit) removes the blinders from our eyes, and peace and contentment fill our days. But in the instant between her gentle touch and the moment

---

[3] Martin Luther King, Jr., from the speech at Memphis in April 1968, just before he was shot.
[4] From the Prayer of St. Francis.

when we really surrender our identity, fear rips through us, and we die. Walking up to the edge is one thing, but dumping our identity over the side is quite another. The rewards are countless, but the courage it takes to do this is immense.

A third thing the Lion must do to save Dorothy, who represents the soul, is draw on **the strength of his friends.** The wisdom of the Scarecrow and the compassion of the Tin Man are his greatest allies. Knowing that they accompany him into the castle is his greatest source of strength.

Courage that is used blindly, without the consultation of our logic and our heart, is more likely a form of bravado than of bravery. Nothing shows off cowardice like recklessness and posturing. Doing a swan dive off a bridge with nothing but a bungie cord between you and death certainly takes guts, but I am not so sure that is bravery. Building bridges between strained relationship and diving head first into our own neurotic patterns is a much bigger act of courage. In the long run, it's much more useful too.

## Wisdom and Courage

*"You are under the unfortunate delusion that simply because you run from danger, you have no courage. You're confusing courage with wisdom."*

—The Wizard of Oz (MGM)

Knowing when to stay and when to flee is an art. Really, it is the key to winning the cosmic poker game of life. In the game of life we are presented with lessons, and the willingness with which we learn those lessons determines the amount of pain and discomfort we experience along the way. As I said in chapter one, it is not a question of whether we get to Kansas. The real question is what the quality of our journey will be like.

The Wizard wisely counsels the Lion, telling him that running from danger is not a lack of courage, but rather an act of wisdom. There are few truths so clearly stated in the movie as this one. Learning to discern the difference between legitimate fear and ego fear is one of the greatest skills we can acquire. This skill, above all others, is a pain saving device as we walk through life.

When people come into my yoga classes, I always give them permission to come out of a pose if they need to. Once they have rested for a bit, they are then encouraged to enter back into the movement with the rest of the class. When people first start getting into their bodies, they seem to have two reactions.

The first reaction is fear. For many westerners, being in the body is a scary thing. For years we are encouraged to deny our physical body—not sleeping enough, eating junk food, and letting the ego fill us with stress. Getting back into the body hurts. It is uncomfortable, not because we are doing something wrong, but because we are starting to assess the damage, and part of that is listening to the body complain. Statements like, "What's wrong with me?" or "I'm not flexible enough," are often heard. For these people, walking into the uncomfortable is the best thing they can do. Their bodies are screaming for some much needed attention, and it takes courage to give it to them.

The other type of response for many people is aggression—the old, "No pain, no gain" approach to the body. Not unlike the first group of people, they see that there are definite problems with the body and dive in head first, trying to solve them. Usually people who try this approach wake up the day after their sadhana[5] with an aching body. People who continue to take this approach often wind up hurting themselves over and over, until they learn that there is another way to be in the body.

This is a great metaphor for life. As we start to take stock of our lives, it can be overwhelming. Not unlike our bodies, our spiritual lives tend to get neglected as well. Once a person realizes this, a path must be chosen. We can recoil in fear or we can try to bulldoze through it. Neither approach will help us at all. At best we will remain at our current level of misery, at worst we will push ourselves into a nervous breakdown.

There is a middle path we can take when it comes to approaching life. It takes the utmost courage and vigilance to walk this path, because it is very narrow[6] and easy to fall off.  Walking this narrow path is the balance between knowing when to stay and when to run—knowing when to push yourself, and when to cut some slack.

In yoga class I call it the edge. The edge is the place we try to reach in our practice where we are a little uncomfortable, yet not in any danger. Sitting at the edge and exploring it allows us to examine what is happening in the pose on a mental, emotional and physical level. Going beyond the edge is not good, because injury is likely to result. Not going right up to the edge, while safe, is not necessarily the best way to get the most out of the pose.

Life is much the same way. We are presented with "poses" all day long—be it the pose of sitting in traffic or the pose of being in a relationship. Some of these life poses last for days and others for just moments. Spirit doesn't ask

---

[5] Sanskrit word meaning spiritual practice. Sadhana can take many forms such as meditation, chanting, service to others etc. In the case of Hatha yoga, sadhana involves breathing (pranayama) and poses (asana).

[6] Matthew 7:14 "For narrow is the gate, and straitened [sic]the way, that leadeth unto life, and few are they that find it."

us to go on suicide missions, but She does ask us to step up to life—to enter into the uncomfortableness of situations and allow Her to help us transcend them.

The Lion's lesson was just that. He needed to discover the subtle difference between backing away from his edge out of common sense, and running away from it out of ignorance. Once he learned this, he began to understand what courage is all about.

This is where our friends Scarecrow and Tin Man come in handy. The Scarecrow gives the Lion a logical assessment of the situation, and the Tin Man allows for that inner knowing to guide. Whatever they say, it is up to the Lion to act. Courage is the motivating agent that propels us forward into the unknown.

There is a story of the Buddha which sums up the balance of wisdom and courage. Siddhartha[7] was crossing the road when a charging elephant drunk with rage, came running toward him. Outrunning the beast would have been a pointless effort and standing still would have been suicide. So Siddhartha extended his left hand in a gesture of compassion and his right hand in a gesture that established a boundary. The elephant came to a halt and knelt down before him.

This story speaks volumes about the wisdom of the Lion and the proper use of courage. The courageous thing to do may be to run or walk, or it may be to stand your ground. What is important to remember is that we must maintain our compassion. Whether we stand our ground or turn and run, we don't need to let hate and malice have their way with us. Compassion can be present in any situation.

---

[7] In Buddhism we are all believed to be potential Buddhas, and many beings are said to have reached this state. Siddhartha is the Buddha who, for lack of a better word founded Buddhism.

Having clear boundaries is also useful. Again, whether or not we run from a situation is not nearly as important as the boundaries we establish for ourselves. Deciding what is acceptable in our lives and then refusing to settle for less, allows us to engage our courage in a meaningful way.

A friend of mine found herself in a bad marriage, and didn't know what to do. She asked me my opinion, and I told her to maintain compassion and establish some boundaries. It would have been easy for her to stay in the marriage and keep on hating him for his walking all over her. The real choice was not about staying or leaving, but rather how she could best love him.

In her case, she chose to stay. For another person it might be appropriate to leave. Courage is most powerful when we can quiet the ego long enough to hear the guidance of Spirit, which allows us to move forward with compassion and integrity.

The *Serenity Prayer*[8] comes to mind when I think of her. Learning to use our courage as a spiritual tool means knowing when to ask for the strength to stay, and knowing when our wisest move is to leave. Knowing the difference, and then acting out of wisdom, is the key.

[8] "God, grant me the serenity to accept the things I cannot change, the courage to change the things I can, and the wisdom to know the difference."

## Chapter Eight

# The Wizard of Oz

*"We hear he is a wiz of a Wiz."*

—Dorothy, Tin Man, Scarecrow & Lion (MGM)

Ever since we were carving our history onto cave walls, human beings have sought answers in religion. Religion has taken many forms, from monotheistic to polytheistic, from patriarchal to matriarchal. Religions have given us some of our most acclaimed art and music, and they have painted some of the darkest chapters in human history.

Whether we like it or not, religion will always be a part of the human experience. Even the atheists have a religion of sorts—science. All religion seeks to fill in the blanks of our "mad lib" understanding of the universe. They attempt to bring reason to what we perceive as chaos. They help us to bring structure to our communities and to define what is right and wrong in our respective cultures.

The Wizard is Dorothy's religion. He gives her hope and inspires her faith. Without him, she would not have bothered to leave Munchkinland. He was, for her, hope and salvation, but in the end he offered her nothing. He was an indispensable empty promise. The Wizard is a paradox. She could not have done it without him, but she never needed him at all.

# A Wizard Who Will Serve

*"If the Wizard is a wizard who will serve."*

—Dorothy (MGM)

As I stated above, we are stuck with religion in some form. Everyone needs something to believe in. Everyone needs to find meaning in life. It is the nature of who we are. Now, the form our individual Wizard may take is entirely up to us—that is, assuming we don't have a political government like Communist China telling us what to believe with a so-called gun to our heads. So if we are going to choose a Wizard to guide us, it might as well be one who will serve us well.

Many religions are not set in place for the betterment of their followers. They are not set up to move believers along their paths, but rather to "load heavy burdens"[1] on their shoulders so that the leaders can have "long and flowing robes" and "seats of honor."[2]

It will serve all seekers well to really look at the religion they belong to—be that a religion of large numbers such as Catholicism and Hinduism, or a more personal relationship with a teacher or guru. Not all those with peaceful demeanors and charismatic personalities are as genuine as they appear.

When I was living in Montana, I wrote an article about *The Church Universal and Triumphant,* which is led by a

---

[1] Matthew 23:4.
[2] Luke 20:46.

woman named Elizabeth Clare Prophet. This group is thought by many of the locals to be a cult. It was interesting to visit their ranch and attend their services, to talk with Ms. Prophet and to learn more about what made this controversial group tick.

Because of the controversy, I decided to investigate just what a cult was, to see if this group fit the bill. I contacted the *Cult Awareness Network* and they sent me all sorts of information. Interestingly, they themselves seemed to embody many of the characteristics of the cults they were trying to warn against. They did, however, identify several qualities that they believe a cult might have. They are: mind control, charismatic leadership, deception, exclusivity, alienation, exploitation, and a totalitarian worldview.

As a result of writing this article, I met a young woman who grew up in *The Church Universal and Triumphant* and had since left. In fact, she was Elizabeth Clare Prophet's daughter. At that point she was following a Taoist path. I asked her what she felt about her mother and the church she had grown up in. Her answer was both amusing and true.

"I have given a lot of thought to the things they say about my mother. Is she manipulative? Sure, but aren't we all. My mother lives in a double-wide trailer on a dusty ranch that looks like a moon crater. If she is doing this for her own personal gain, she certainly hasn't gained much.

"As far as the cult thing goes, there are lots of groups who fit that cult definition a lot more closely than *The Church Universal and Triumphant*—the Catholic Church for one. People seem to forget that 2,000 years ago a very charismatic man came telling people to leave their jobs and homes and follow him. Did that make Jesus a cult leader?"

She had some interesting points. I have to admit, the beliefs of Ms. Prophet's group are very unique. I do not share them for myself, but they are no more outrageous than believing that Mary was a Virgin or that Moses parted the Red Sea. The only difference is that this group is smaller in numbers, so they are easier to pick on.

I do not bring this up to defend the beliefs or actions of *The Church Universal and Triumphant*. I bring it up because the size and shape of a group has little or nothing to do with its effectiveness in helping us find Kansas. The question that needs to be asked is this: Does this church or minister or guru have the best interests of the follower in mind, or is this person or group of people a bunch of greedy control freaks? Is this a Wizard who will serve or one who will suck the life force out of us?

I believe that it is not for me to decide who or what a person follows. If something is working, then by all means—keep doing it. If it is not, then don't walk, run! Finding a Wizard who will serve must be the responsibility of the seeker.

The Wizard is there to serve the follower, not the other way around. This is not to say that spiritual leaders don't deserve our respect. But working for Spirit is an honor. It doesn't make you special and it doesn't entitle you to privileges. A true teacher or spiritual institution puts the students first, and is willing to lay down everything for the betterment of even one student.

Being a Wizard should not be about self glory, but rather about the glory of what is true—-that we are all expressions of God and that within each being is unlimited potential. He should never threaten to withdraw his love or his support and should always speak truth. His power should come from God, rather than from bells and whistles, smoke and mirrors.

His job is not to do something for us, but to inspire us to keep pressing on along the yellow brick road. His finger should never point toward himself as an answer, but rather toward the inner wisdom that is inherent in all beings.

These things apply as much to the Pope as they do to Elizabeth Clare Prophet. They hold true as much for the Guru-disciple relationship as they do for the entire Muslim faith. The Wizard, whether in the form of a person, a group of people, or an institution, must be in place to serve. Anything more than that will be nothing but a millstone tied around our necks.[3]

Even those who follow a scientific path should explore the intentions of their Wizard. We now have the capacity to clone. Does this mean we should do it? Are all the things we do in the name of science really for the betterment of people, or do they actually keep us back?

While science has provided us with better and better ways of treating serious illnesses such as cancer, it has also given us pesticides to spray on our foods, which many experts believe are the cause of many of our illnesses. On the one hand science has given us the ability to send a man to the moon, but it has not yet given us the ability to travel to the distant reaches of our mind.

It is easy to attack religions and gurus. Finding fault with them is usually not hard. They are human institutions and human beings, which means they have all the qualities of humanity. They struggle and grow; they change and evolve. Learning to grow with them and to be a part of that growth is up to us. Knowing when one particular Wizard is no longer serving is the key. At that point change can occur, or the relationship can be severed.

I used to do a lot of Catholic bashing. In their eyes

---

[3] Matthew 18:6.

I was a sinner, no longer worthy of fully celebrating their Mass with them. On countless levels I disagreed with them and found myself getting angry whenever I would see the Pope in his little bullet-proof car. I then realized that all my anger was in vain. When I accepted that the Roman Catholic Church was serving millions of people, and that I had a choice about what role, if any, this institution would play in my life, I felt free. It was no longer my Wizard because it no longer served me. It was not until I forgave them that I was able to go off and find another, more healthy form of the Wizard to bring structure to my life.

## The Small and the Meek

> "The beneficent Oz has every intention of granting your requests, but first you must prove yourselves worthy by performing a very small task. Bring me the broomstick of the Witch of the West."
>
> —The Wizard (MGM)

Now having said all that, I am going to shift gears in what will seem to be an unexpected direction. Now I would like to turn my attention to the seeker and try to find out exactly what is the proper role for the seeker in relation to the Wizard.

When Dorothy and her friends visit the Wizard, they come with a great deal of humility. They recognize that this man has something they want and that it is through humility that they will get it. This is another paradox. On the one hand it is the Wizard who is here to serve the seeker, but it is the seeker who needs to be humbled. Therefore it is about trust and faith.

When the Wizard says, "bring me the broomstick. . . ,"

there is no room for discussion. The rules are set forth and Dorothy can choose to see the game through, or she can go find another Wizard. This is where the need for trust and humility comes in, and why a wise and well informed choice needs to be made before one starts his or her relationship with any religion, teacher or guru.

I remember hearing the Pope speak once about being Roman Catholic in relationship to many of the controversial issues such as abortion, birth control and homosexuality that always seem to accompany any discussion about religion. He said that to be Catholic was to follow the teachings of Rome and to adhere to its principles and not to make up your own rules as you went along.

At first I was bothered by his statements, but then I realized that I agreed with him very much. Not about his views on abortion and homosexuality, but on choosing a path that is right and then following it with passion and commitment. He was not saying that everyone should be Catholic, but rather saying that if you are going to call yourselves Catholic you should adhere to the teachings that define what a Catholic is.

Because I don't agree with making another human being infallible or telling a woman what to do with her own body, I am no longer a Catholic. I have my own path now that involves the practice of yoga, the study of the Bible and occasional visits to a local Episcopal parish. The Wizard I follow is mine by choice, but because I have made that choice, I try to follow that path with passion, commitment and humility.

When yoga asks me to practice non-violence[4], I listen and I do not question it, even if I would rather give someone the finger for cutting me off on the highway. When Jesus

---

[4] *Ahimsa* is part of the eight limbs of Raja Yoga. It is the practice of not harming, or non-violence.

asks me to offer my aggressor the other cheek, I do my best to do that rather than using their aggression as a justification for my own attack. I do these things willingly because I have chosen my path, and I believe it is a path that will serve me if I follow it mindfully. I know that the time-tested teachings of the New Testament and of Yoga offer me freedom even if I feel unwilling to practice them at the time. I do my best to humble myself enough to follow these things and trust they will continue to work in my life.

Is my path the best path? For me perhaps, but certainly not for everyone else. Do I practice it perfectly? Hardly, but I do keep returning to it, and I know that when I am walking with my Wizard, life seems to go much more smoothly. When I drift from my path, things get mucky. Life is not always easy when I humble myself and follow my Wizard, but it is always easier in the long run than doing it my own way, and each time I do so, I draw a step closer to home.

We are all given a Wizard at birth. Traditionally it is the Wizard our parents gave us—be it religious, secular, or something destructive like drug addiction. As we move into adulthood we have more of a choice. We can choose something traditional, such as a larger religion, or we can choose something non-traditional like the eclectic paths that seem to be springing forth from the new age movement. We can also choose something with no overt spiritual overtones, such as intellectual studies. My friend Mike used to feel spiritually nourished by figuring out complex physics equations.

Whatever it is that we choose, it should be something that we are willing to follow. We don't need to follow blindly but with humility, and trust that this path is the one that will help to clear away all the blocks to the awareness of our true power. The Wizard did nothing for Dorothy except point to the things she least wanted to look at, such as the Witch's castle. And that is exactly what any good Wizard should do.

# The Land of "E PLURIBUS UNUM"

*"Times being what they were, I accepted the job [as wizard], retaining the balloon against the advent of a quick getaway. And in that balloon, my dear Dorothy, you and I will return to the land of E Pluribus Unum!"*

—The Wizard of Oz (MGM)

It is common knowledge that there are two basic causes of war, money and religion. Both are based in fear and the belief in scarcity. There is no need for a lack of resources on this planet, but fear is what drives our economy, so rather than share, we spill blood because someone came up with the silly notion that killing is somehow easier than sharing.

Equally absurd is the notion that one person or group of people can be favored in the eyes of God. The chosen people are not special because God has chosen them, but because they have chosen God—and not a God that is limited by a simplistic definition, but rather a God that is so far reaching that no definition could hold him/her.

People heading up the religious right in the United States do not understand this, nor do the Muslim fundamentalists and extreme orthodox Jews in the Middle East. They have all tried to put God in a very small and narrow box. It can never work. Omnipresence cannot be contained in a book or a religion or style of prayer. It is beyond time and space and therefore beyond any temporal conceptions we might try to come up with.

The truth of God, which is in essence the truth about who we are, is magnificent and will never fit into words. It cannot be explained or described but it can be experienced. And in that experience God is realized.

As we have been discussing, the Wizard represents the outward expression of Spirit or religion. He has an important role, but he is not clean. He, like all our thoughts, has been filtered through the ego—both the ego of individuals and the collective or group ego that develops in any group. Because of this, no Wizard is really pure. There are elements of truth in what he says and does, but he is still a very human creation.

Gandhi's idea that all true religions are different paths leading to the same place is very true. If you really follow the teachings of any of the great masters, you are sure to find God. Whether you practice the eight-fold path of Buddhism, keep the Commandments of Moses, or participate in Native American vision quests, you will experience God, and when you do you will find truth and compassion.

There is something to be said for following a set path. As I said, my practice of studying the New Testament and practicing yoga is perfect for me, but at the end of the journey I will be sitting with the lady who found her truth chanting mantras, or with the guy who danced in circles.[5] Spiritual traditions are a means to the realization of the sublime.

We are not valuable because we are a member of a certain group or because we call God by a certain name. We are not valuable because we follow a guru or observe a certain diet. We are valuable because we are a spark of the divine. And the only thing Gurus, priests, rabbis and elders can do for us is point us back in the direction of home, and home is, of course, within.

Once Dorothy and Toto confront the Wizard, there is a moment of reckoning where they realize that the Wizard

---

[5] Whirling Dervishes.

is a "very good man, [he's] just a very bad Wizard."[6] It is out of this reckoning that the Wizard is able to take a few genuine moments with his new friends and really do what he wanted to do all along—inspire people. It was in doing this that he reminded Scarecrow that he really was smart, showed Tin Man that he did have a heart, and acknowledged the Lion for his bravery.

This is the first step in getting our religions and spiritual leaders to really serve us. We must look behind the curtain and see that most of religion is nothing more than smoke and mirrors. Religion was created by humans, and when we become mindful of that we free our spiritual leader up to be a server.

Sometimes I will go out dancing at a night club here in San Francisco. It is interesting to see how many of my students will see me there and react in shock—as if I am doing something wrong. They have this image of what a yoga instructor should be and do, and it is very unrealistic. What's more, would you really want to seek spiritual guidance from someone who lives in denial of their humanity?

Once we free the Wizard by confronting his facade, he is free to "return to the land of E Pluribus Unum." "E pluribus Unum" is Latin for, "out of the many, one." When we strip away the bells and whistles from the "many" religions, we begin to find "one" truth. Again, this one truth is nothing that can be put into words, but it can be experienced.

This experience of truth will never come from name calling and holy wars. It will not come until we stop using our Bibles and Korans as weapons and start using them to cast our minds in the direction of Truth. Once we do so, we

---

[6] MGM.

find that we become chosen people not because of our religious affiliation, but because of our ruby slippers. And in the end it is the slippers, not the Wizard, that will bring us home.

# The Return Home

*"She had to find it in herself. Now those magic slippers will take you home in two seconds."*

—Glinda, *Good Witch of the North* (MGM)

And so, in the end, we are faced with one last paradox. When we walk the yellow brick road, we are not traveling to a place in time and space. There is no map, only a few sign posts. The spiritual journey along the yellow brick road is to our truth.

It is about learning that all the power in the universe is at our feet, and with a little bit of wisdom, an open heart and a lot of courage, we can go home any time we choose. The spiritual journey is more of a coming of age and a ripening of our soul than a set of hurdles which we need to jump through. It is "a journey without distance"[1] but an adventure none the less.

In the end, we learn the same lesson that Dorothy learned through her experience in Oz.

*Well, I think it wasn't enough to want to see Uncle Henry and Auntie Em. And it's that if I ever go looking for my heart's desire again, I won't look any farther than my own backyard. Because if it isn't there, I never really lost it to begin with.*[2]

---

[1] *A Course in Miracles.*
[2] MGM.

When we reach the end of our journey, we find ourselves in a quandary—stay in the dream, or wake up to reality. Staying in the dream is not really an option, though we can drag our feet and hit the psychological snooze button for a very long time. And so we say our good-byes and click our heels, and we wake up to find that all we ever loved about Oz was waiting for us in Kansas.

All the love we share in this world is as eternal as we are—every expression of kindness, every good deed—all of the friendships and all of the generosity. They all follow us home. The only things that get left behind are the fear, the darkness, and the emptiness.

When we arrive in Kansas, there will not be much to say. Our adventure, if we really live it, will be a surreal and wild ride filled with highs and lows, joy and sorrow, love and fear. But through it all, we will grow in breadth as well as depth, and our understanding of ourselves will grow too. In short, we will find contentment, and that is what Kansas is all about.

So here in this moment, each of us is presented with a choice—the only choice there ever was, and the only choice there ever will be. We can muster up our wisdom, compassion and courage and click our heels, or we can stand here looking at the sky waiting for some external wizard to zip us off in a balloon filled with a lot of hot air. I guess it's not much of a choice after all.

So there is just one thing left to say. I think Dorothy summed it up when she exclaimed, "Oh Toto! There's no place like home!"

# Oz Resources

Baum, L. Frank: *The Wizard of Oz*. North South Books, 1996.

Bousky, Samuel: *The Wizard of Oz Revealed*. Writers' Consortium, 1995.

Green, Joey: *The Zen of Oz: Ten Spiritual Lessons from over the Rainbow*. Renaissance Books, 1998

Maguire, Gregory: *Wicked: The Life and Times of the Wicked Witch of the West*. HarperCollins, NY 1996

# General Resources

The Holy Bible, New International Version International Bible Society, 1984

Bruce, Lenny: *How to Talk Dirty and Influence People: An Autobiography*. Simon & Schuster, 1992.

*A Course in Miracles*. Second edition, The Foundation for Inner Peace, 1992.

*Gospel of Thomas* from *The Nag Hammadi Library*, ed. James M. Robinson, Harper & Row, 1981.

Jeffers, Susan, *Feel the Fear and Do it Anyway*, Fawcett Books, 1992.

Millman, Dan: *Way of the Peaceful Warrior*. H.J. Kramer Inc., 1984.

*Oxford Dictionary of World Religions*, ed. John Bowker, Oxford University Press, 1997.

*Peace Pilgrim: Her Life and Work in Her Own Words*, Ocean Tree Books, 1991.

# Web Sites

www.darrenmain.com
My website is filled with links to other spiritual resources on the net. You can also get a current schedule of my classes, workshops and retreats, as well as review some of my other writing.

www.castroyoga.com
The website for Castro Yoga, the yoga studio founded by David Nelson and me.

www.eskimo.com/~tiktok
A site filled with information on Oz books, the movie and much more.

www.literature.org/authors/baum-l-frank/the-wonderful-wizard-of-oz/
You can read Frank Baum's book on line, broken down chapter by chapter.

# Index

FINDHORN
*Press*

Findhorn Press is the publishing business of the Findhorn Community which has grown around the Findhorn Foundation in northern Scotland.

For further information about the Findhorn Foundation and the Findhorn Community, please contact:

Findhorn Foundation
The Visitors Centre
The Park, Findhorn IV36 3TZ, Scotland, UK
tel 01309 690311• fax 01309 691301
email reception@findhorn.org
www.findhorn.org

For a complete Findhorn Press catalogue, please contact:

Findhorn Press

| | |
|---|---|
| The Park, Findhorn, | P. O. Box 13939 |
| Forres IV36 3TY | Tallahassee |
| Scotland, UK | Florida 32317-3939, USA |
| Tel 01309 690582 | Tel (850) 893 2920 |
| freephone 0800-389 9395 | toll-free 1-877-390-4425 |
| Fax 01309 690036 | Fax (850) 893 3442 |

e-mail info@findhornpress.com
findhornpress.com

Mary Bassano works as a color-music therapist and teaches classes on how to use color, music, and other metaphysical concepts to bring about a balanced life. She spent two years at Oberlin Conservatory of Music and has worked as a social case worker for various county and state child welfare agencies. Combining her social-work skills with her musical background, she became a music therapist in a large hospital.